The Psychology of the Yogas

Gidi Ifergan

equinox

SHEFFIELD UK BRISTOL CT

Published by Equinox Publishing Ltd.

UK: Office 415, The Workstation, 15 Paternoster Row, Sheffield, South Yorkshire S1 2BX

USA: ISD, 70 Enterprise Drive, Bristol, CT 06010

www.equinoxpub.com

First published 2021

ISBN-13 978 1 80050 086 0 (hardback)
978 1 80050 087 7 (paperback)
978 1 80050 088 4 (ePDF)
978 1 80050 125 6 (ePub)

British Library Cataloguing-in-Publication Data

A catalogue record for this book is available from the British Library.

Library of Congress Cataloging-in-Publication Data

Names: Ifergan, Gidi, author.
Title: The psychology of the yogas / Gidi Ifergan.
Description: Sheffield, South Yorkshire ; Bristol, CT : Equinox Publishing Ltd, 2021. | Includes bibliographical references and index. | Summary: "The Psychology of the Yogas explores the dissonance between the promises of the yogic quest and psychological states of crisis"—Provided by publisher.
Identifiers: LCCN 2021001959 (print) | LCCN 2021001960 (ebook) | ISBN 9781800500860 (hardback) | ISBN 9781800500877 (paperback) | ISBN 9781800500884 (epdf) | ISBN 9781800501256 (epub)
Subjects: LCSH: Yoga. | Psychology.
Classification: LCC B132.Y6 I34 2021 (print) | LCC B132.Y6 (ebook) | DDC 181/.45019—dc23
LC record available at https://lccn.loc.gov/2021001959
LC ebook record available at https://lccn.loc.gov/2021001960

Typeset by JS Typesetting Ltd, Porthcawl, Mid Glamorgan

Contents

Foreword vii
About the Author ix

Introduction 1

1 The Psychological Layers in Patañjali's Yoga 19

2 *Pratipakṣa Bhāvanā*: Cultivating the Opposite 45

3 *Pratipakṣa Bhāvanā* as Imagining the Opposite 71

4 Western Psychology as a Temporary Complement to Yoga 87

5 Between Classical Yoga and Dzogchen 109

6 The Psychology of Tibetan Dzogchen: Ati Yoga 121

Epilogue 141

Glossary 147
Notes 155
Bibliography 167
Index 173

The Psychology of the Yogas

Foreword

Patañjali's *Yoga Sūtras* is a crowning jewel in India's unexcelled tradition of scientific contemplative inquiry. The brilliance and transcultural relevance of Patañjali's formalization of yoga psychology is attested to by the fact that his aphorisms have been richly interpreted within theistic, monotheistic, monist, non-dual and non-theistic systems of philosophy and practice.

The truth is that many of the foundational structures of modern Western psychotherapy were discovered millennia ago by ancient yogis in the depths of their contemplations: concepts of habit formation, instinctual drives, subliminal imprinting, behavioral consequences (*karma-phala*), attachment theory, ego psychology and positive psychology, to name a few. Moreover, these deep psychological structures were revealed as constituting a yoga psychology that seamlessly transitions beyond the workings of the psyche into a mystical and transcendental domain that has the potential to release the human mind from all forms of suffering and restriction. Indeed, Patañjali's *Yoga Sūtras*, which date back to the third century CE, are virtually a transcendental CBT (cognitive behavior therapy).

This splendid study by Dr. Ifergan continues to extend Patañjali's yoga by presenting it in its intended scope; as a praxis for deep psychological healing that is complete within itself, and which has the capacity to purify and transform the human mind, revealing its ultimate and liberated essence as the true-Self.

Drawing on his own decades long, compassionate engagement with Indian yoga and Tibetan Dzogchen, Dr. Ifergan explores the full contours and scope of Patañjali's integral yoga, including Patañjali's higher order insights into the nature of conditioning, the yoga methods for deep healing and purification, and the peaks of yogic realization.

A particular virtue of this study is its presentation of Patañjali in settings that can be easily recognized by readers who have engaged in any form of psychotherapy or meditation, or who are simply reflecting deeply about their emotional lives. Psychologists, counsellors and psychotherapists who are looking to ground their work in a knowledge of yoga psychology, and its far-reaching potential, will be richly rewarded in these pages. Certainly, readers who practice yoga with a knowledge of Patañjali's eight-stage (*aṣṭāṅga*) system will benefit immensely from the attention given to practices such as "cultivating the opposite" and the use of creative imagination in yoga psychology.

The final chapters of this study show how the depth psychology of yoga can be framed and enriched with insights drawn from the famous fourteenth-century Tibetan scholar-yogi Longchenpa. The inclusion of non-dual Dzogchen allows Dr. Ifergan to present a holistic approach to cultivating a sustained, embodied *and* socially responsible disengagement from instinctive drives and impulses. The Dzogchen principles of naturalness, non-action, simplicity and spontaneous, acausal realization, effortlessly reveal the same space of unconditioned, immanent awareness that is sought through classical yoga practice.

Dr. Ifergan shows how the results-level yoga of Dzogchen can deepen and enrich the more programmatic repertoire of traditional eight-stage yoga by providing direct, immediate access to our ever-present, natural state of unbounded awareness.

The potential of the present moment to reveal our primordial unconditioned state, invites practitioners to enter the formalities of yoga practice (personal morality, postures and breath, affective detachment, meditation and transcendental absorption), free of strategy and grasping at outcomes.

In this way, a yoga practice that's developed with a firm discipline and an incremental deconditioning of primitive patterning, reactive emotions and conceptual attachment, is infused with flashes of spontaneous release into transcendent awareness; moments of full realization that punctuate the path, and purify the very imprints and programming that entrap us.

Dr. Peter Fenner
Author of Radiant Mind *and* Natural Awakening
November 2020

About the Author

Dr. Gidi Ifergan is an author and a researcher of Indian philosophy and Tibetan Buddhism at Monash University in Melbourne, Australia. He is the author of *The Man from Samyé: Longchenpa on Praxis, Its Negation and Liberation* (2014), *Negation and Liberation in Longchenpa's Teachings* (2015, in Hebrew) and *Self-discovery in the Psychology of Yoga* (2018, in Hebrew).

Ifergan teaches yoga and meditation in different frameworks, such as beginner and advanced teacher training at the Victorian Institute of Yoga Education and Teacher Training in Melbourne, home-studio classes, workshops in Israel and Australia, and E-VAM Institute's Buddhist summer schools.

He has undertaken extensive studies of Dzogchen teachings in Tibetan Buddhism; participated in retreats with Dzogchen master Chögyal Namkhai Norbu in Australia, Israel and Italy from 1992 to 2018; and studied classic forms of Indian yoga with Master Shri Brahma Gopal Bhaduri and his senior disciple Shri Shiv Shankar Tripathi, which included travels to Varanasi, India from 1994 to 2003.

He is an accomplished classical guitarist. He has released two albums with Cala Records (UK): *Vast Expanse* (2016) and *Down Celestial Avenue* (2018). His music has attracted complimentary reviews and has been featured on ABC Classic FM, Byron Bay FM, and is offered as the inflight entertainment of several airlines.

Introduction

The seeds of my intention to study the psychology of yoga developed when I read testimonies of Western yoga practitioners who had embarked upon spiritual quests and spent substantial periods, sometimes over twelve years, in India or the Himālayas practicing yoga and meditation under the guidance of a guru. As a result, they reported profound and ongoing experiences of love and compassion, clarity and lucidity, visions of deities, an incredible sense of openness, good health, etc. In short, they reported sublime experiences that represented the peaks of fulfillment in their spiritual quests. What I found to be intriguing was that, despite the wisdom and insights derived from the heightened states of mind they had experienced, when they returned to the West after all those years spent in Asia, they reported immense difficulties and crises in areas like their work and family lives, their intimate relationships, health and money. Such testimonies invoked the question of why practitioners who had such sublime experiences touching the heights of yoga and meditation still suffered such states of crisis. Paradoxically, practice at that level of profundity is supposed to liberate one from distress and painful circumstances. That is to say, although they were spiritually evolved, to my wonder they had become psychologically unresolved and unsettled.

Traditional Indian and Tibetan Buddhist teachers and the seminal works of these traditions bear an unspoken condition as a promise: If one is to practice yoga and meditation with a teacher diligently and with commitment to the Dharma as the holistic "right way to live," one will be liberated from the stress and pain that results from inner conflicts, negative self-perceptions, destructive patterns of behavior and subliminal mental imprints that dictate one's life. Dharma includes the duties, rituals, laws, conduct and virtues as prescribed in the different Indian philosophical schools and branches of yoga, including Buddhism, that their followers aspire to abide by.

The question of the promises of yoga versus times of psychological crisis that occur along the path was invoked again when I met a friend of mine, Dr. Nimrod Sheinman, a reputable professional in the field of integrative therapeutics, who for decades attended annual meditation workshops and retreats. During these retreats, he would either sit as a participant, or assist in managing the registration and the kitchen. As such, he had encounters with many returning participants, as well as conversations with many newcomers. When I asked him whether he could recall participants that had undergone a significant psychological transformation, he answered without hesitation that during all those years, through about thousands of meditators, many had meaningful experiences and insights but rarely a lasting transformation outcome.

Later on, I came across an article by Jack Engler: "Promises and Perils of the Spiritual Path."[1] Engler, a clinical psychologist and practicing Buddhist, conducted a Rorschach study of *vipassanā* meditators before and after a three-month retreat. He found that personal issues are not healed simply by meditation or other forms of spiritual practice alone. Specific problems, such as anger, depression, early abuse, addictions, trust, intimacy, etc., all require particular attention and more than likely a professional or communal intervention toward their healing. He states that these issues "can't be resolved simply by watching the moment-to-moment flow of thought, feelings and sensation in the mind. These problems arise in a relationship; they have to be healed in relationship."[2]

In considering the testimonies of the aforementioned Western yoga practitioners, the conversation with my friend, and Jack Engler's findings, I have found a tension between the promises of the spiritual quest and psychological states of crisis, despite the prolonged and profound experiences of compassion and clarity that occur on the path of yoga. This dissonance has enhanced my curiosity even further and has driven me to undertake the current study: exploring and clarifying the friction between the promises of the spiritual path and the psychological issues that may occur along that path. This is a study conducted with regard to the framework of yoga psychology and the methods it offers for practitioners to heal and resolve their psychological issues.

Those who speak in praise of yoga tend to emphasize poses, breathing and meditation, rather than the yoga of the psyche and its world of feelings and emotions. The interest in yoga has instigated a wave of curiosity about its historical, cultural and philosophical origins. This, in turn, has raised a larger question: How can the origins of yoga, rooted in such an ancient and distant culture, be understood in contemporary Western culture? In order to satisfy the immense interest in yoga, various systems have been developed to train yoga teachers. These systems mostly teach the physical aspect of yoga, the *āsanas*, and although at times they may include the history and philosophy of yoga, the study of the psychological dimension of yoga as an autonomous theme, based on both theory and practice, is often overlooked.

This book offers a study of the mental and psychological dimensions of yoga and examines the role emotions play within it. Yoga practitioners are confronted with emotional challenges. At times, they act and react compulsively, out of their emotions and out of identification with their inner narratives. In addition to exploring the psychological theory of yoga and the attitudes, values and beliefs that the yogi is encouraged to adopt and cultivate, I will focus on yoga's concrete and practical psychological methods. These methods are psychotherapeutic; they have the power to free yoga practitioners from identifications that solidify their day-to-day existential self (personality), the identifications that perpetuate vicious cycles of suffering. In this book I will sketch out the outlines of these methods.

My main source is the *Yoga Sūtras*. This text, written by the sage Patañjali in the third century CE, outlines a deep psychological foundation that provides a key to understanding the human psyche. The text was written in concise, condensed verses. Due to their terse style, their discussion of feelings and emotions is limited. In most cases, the verses do not provide clear meanings of moods, temperaments or mental attitudes, nor how to work with them. Perhaps this stems from Patañjali's choice to address his work to that archetypal yogic figure of Vedic culture that was brought to India between about 1500 and 1000 BCE by tribes that arrived from the north, named the Aryans—"the noble ones" (a concept adopted and distorted by the Nazis). The Vedic culture was constituted of a collection of hymns and other ancient religious texts dedicated to certain deities. That is, it was founded on the Veda, the "body of knowledge" that established a sacred world by means of hymns, sounds and language addressed to deities.

The archetypal yogic figure of Vedic culture is that long-haired, bearded, silent ascetic Keśin, who lives in the forest, far from any social framework. He is the advanced yogi who, according to the *Ṛgveda*, a sacred collection of Vedic Sanskrit hymns, can "fly on the wings of the Self."[3] He is described in the Keśin Hymn from the *Ṛgveda*:

> The long-haired one carries within himself fire and poison and earth. To look at him is like seeing heavenly brightness in it said to be light itself ... The sages, girdled with the wind, are clad in dust of yellow hue. They follow the path of the wind when the gods have penetrated them ... Uplifted by our sagehood we have ascended upon the winds. You mortals see just our bodies ... The sage flies through the inner region, illuminating all forms below. Dedicated to holy work he is a friend of every god ... Being the wind's horse, the friend of Vayu and god-inspired, the sage is at home in both oceans, the Eastern and the Western ... Wandering in the track of celestial beings and sylvan beasts, the long-haired one, knowing their aspiration, is a sweet and most uplifting friend.[4]

This hymn revolves around central themes of yoga: the profound pure silence (*mauna*), the soaring between Heaven and Earth, and the encounter with the gods, all themes that are directly connected to stilling the mind and the manifestations of supernatural powers. It seems to me that Patañjali had such a yogi in mind when he composed his own text, one who is at a highly advanced stage of yoga practice and engaged in a pure and deep form of highly concentrated meditation with access to its mysterious powers. Since, in the case of the advanced yogi, behavior and psychological experiences did not create obstacles on the path of yoga, there was no need to discuss them extensively.

Patañjali's instructions to adopt demanding moral codes of conduct demonstrate his awareness of the social interactions of a yoga disciple. Family and social relationships may be demanding for yoga practitioners. They may put them in a situation in which their desires and the need for security, order and love clash with those of others. Such friction, in turn, is liable to generate conflict, both internally—within the psyche of practitioners—as well as externally, as part of their everyday life. In such situations, practitioners are exposed to tensions that generate feelings and emotions that may challenge their fixed beliefs and cause them to act out.

Social interactions are capable of mirroring how quiet the yoga practitioner's mind has become, to what extent mental contents have been emptied or resolved, whether the subliminal emotional or mental triggers have been deactivated, or how love and compassion are manifested as a natural expression in action.

As I write this, my gaze turns to the vast expanses seen out of the window where the silent long-haired yogi abides, hovering between Heaven and Earth. But at the same time, I seek the possibilities that Patañjali offers yoga students, those involved in social interaction, committed here on Earth.

Accounts of yoga by yoga practitioners and teachers often highlight and describe the transcendental and mystical dimension of their experiences and the state of liberation as Self-realization. However, these texts tell only part of the spiritual yogic journey. They do not address difficulties such as depression, the disintegration of relationships, livelihood problems or other difficulties that may arise after the extraordinary experiences have faded away.

Because of the attitudes, values and beliefs that a yoga student is required to adopt and nurture—friendship, non-violence, compassion—he will find it difficult to admit to himself as well as to others when his habitual tendencies and behaviors or ideas collide with basic yogic values and beliefs. The absence of such honesty can intensify an internal conflict in which the ego is hidden and concealed and remains captive to its self-image. After all, who really wants to confront pain, dissatisfaction and self-disappointment? To quote T. S. Eliot, "Humankind cannot bear very much reality."[5]

The key to resolving internal conflicts is, first and foremost, self-honesty. But it seems that for most yoga practitioners, the cultivation of self-honesty is not obvious. After all, they are supposed to transcend jealousy, anger, desire and all other emotions perceived as enemies, because there is nothing between such enemies and the true Self. Often, the desire to transcend emotions results in their denial or suppression, instead of leading to the cultivation of an unshakable equanimity or sense of contentment. Spiritual or mystical insight can have a powerful impact, but it does not necessarily transform someone who has had such an experience into a mature adult. Neither does such an experience automatically cause one to behave morally and appropriately. One is still exposed to daily life challenges, whether associated with sex, relationships, work or money, which, under certain circumstances, can ignite a sequence of emotions that have the potential to distort or blind one's perspective.

These volatile triggers are nothing but the overpowering mental imprints that are dormant and etched in one's mind as recorded reactions to various events or objects. These imprints translate into subliminal self-perception. For example, a child that was continually bullied at school can develop subliminal self-perceptions such as "I am a victim," or "I am unwanted," which then become mental imprints. When triggered, even in adulthood, they can stir emotions such as shame, anger or a sense of rejection and lead him to act them out, or at times even look for compensation for such emotions to ease them. In another example, a person drives back home. He is relaxed and enjoying listening to a beautiful guitar prelude. Another driver aggressively overtakes him without indicating, triggering a dormant mental imprint that may be: "I am transparent," stirring an aggressive reaction in response. Such a reaction, in certain instances, can even escalate and become dangerous to the safety of both of them. These subliminal and dormant self-perceptions are like seeds, that when given the right conditions of light, water and soil have the power to germinate.

These imprints are located in between the layers of the mind, and they may be stirred up in reaction to various stimuli, compelling one to act out in reaction to the emotional charge they generate. Yoga does not relate directly to the causes of psychological suffering characteristic to contemporary Western culture, such as anxiety, trauma, depression, loneliness and issues concerning self-esteem, mourning, parenting, relationships, addictions and codependency. For this reason, we must reexamine the psychological methods and their therapeutic functions in classical yoga with the aim of neutralizing mental imprints. That is to say, we aim at deactivating their potential to trigger and cause us to act out, thereby defusing their emotional charge, which distorts the perception of reality and brings about suffering.

One of the main questions concerns the concept of *pratipakṣa bhāvanā*, a practice of cultivating and imagining the opposite, which I will consider as a psychotherapeutic method that can assist yoga practitioners to navigate the course of their yoga journey. In the Western world, yoga has been commercialized. Today it is mainly focused on the body and its images, blended with New Age methods that have made it into a spiritual bypass for some practitioners;[6] that is, they use yoga practice in order to bypass or avoid confronting threatening or disturbing feelings. Some practitioners who focus on self-transcendence dive into the seductive world of contemplation and are captivated by the idea of avoiding emotions, which they sometimes consider to be the enemies of yoga. In an attempt to transcend their basic emotional needs, they fail to recognize their message and value.

However, practitioners need to be aware of emotions, and they must cultivate a healthy mind devoid of obsessions, compulsive behaviors, addictions and anxiety. They must develop a good sense of self and long-lasting personal relationships, so that their emotional balance is not disturbed or distracted by emotions such as anger, love and jealousy. A healthy mind provides a solid psychological basis for the inner discipline required for practicing yoga and meditation.

As I consider this, I am curious and drawn to the expanses seen through the window, and to the silent long-haired yogi. This attraction is a movement of thought that originates from an imprint etched in my mind, a response to a deep wish to fulfill the aspirations of mind, a desire resulting from their absence. Nevertheless, embarking on the path of yoga in itself is rooted in a mental imprint, the inner wish to come face to face with the Self, to abide within the Self.

From a yogic point of view, this attraction is positive, but it is also one of the infinite movements occurring in the mind that range from attraction to rejection. For the yogi who has realized the wisdom that discerns between the world of phenomena and the real Self, all the mental and emotional movements are nothing but suffering. This, according to Patañjali's verse, seems radically counterintuitive.[7]

I remember the precious moments of the birth of my children, yet these very memories, according to Patañjali, are part of those movements of thoughts and emotions that prevent the individual to recognize their natural, real Self. Thus, this type of precious memory is also a source of tension, for it may become an obstacle to the realization of one's true Self, which is a Self emptied of all content. Due to such tension, the yoga practitioner's gaze is redirected to the interiority of his mind in which movements of thought and emotion are generated from the infinite field of the subjugating mental imprints. Such an in-depth gaze is crucial, as it enables a growing knowledge of the practitioner's true nature, expressed as a stream of insights that enhance healing and allow liberation.

Like the four truths of the Buddha, who is the *vaidyarāja* (king of healers), according to Buddhist tradition, Patañjali's yoga also offers a paradigm of healing.[8] *Duḥkha* (suffering, dissatisfaction, frustration) is the first of the four fundamental truths of Buddhism. The second truth is the *tṛṣṇā*, according to which the cause of pain is the craving, the thirst for the certain, the safe, the pleasurable and the eternal. It is a mental movement that generates a subjective sense of being a solid, continuous, real ego that is nothing more than a collection of habitual tendencies and impressions. Thus, one acts out of identification with one's belief system, feelings and emotions, and one's involvement and attachment to events, situations and phenomena in everyday life. Moreover, this ego protects itself on both the conscious and subconscious levels, thereby solidifying and sustaining the craving for safety, certainty and pleasure, and the tendency to avoid situations of sorrow and pain. According to the third truth, *nirodha*, it is possible to put an end to suffering and resolve it, and the fourth truth, *mārga*, the "noble eightfold path," is the means to do so. Ultimately, the purpose of this path is to lead the aspirant toward the realization of his true nature, thereby putting an end to his misconceptions and pains. Like the dreamer who realizes that his nightmare was only a dream, the aspirant after liberation experiences a profound insight that doubly frees him, both from the mistaken perception of the dream as a concrete reality and from the anxiety of the nightmare itself.

The long-haired silent one proclaims the light and rides on the wind free from *duḥkha*. I do not know whether he will come again and when, because it is impossible to anticipate his arrival or to impose anything on him or on original awareness. If expectations or anything else could have been imposed on him, or on pure awareness, again freedom from duḥkha would have been bound.

The friction between the anticipation and the actual face-to-face acquaintance with the true Self brings me to Vyāsa, the first commentator of the *Yoga Sūtras*, who clarified the therapeutic principle at the heart of yoga, and whose commentary is essential to the understanding of the text. Vyāsa is thought to have lived close to the time of Patañjali in the fifth century. His approach suggests that the therapeutic method of yoga is similar to the method used in medicine, based on the diagnosis of the disease (*roga*), on the identification of the cause of the disease (*roga-hetu*), on the understanding that it is possible to cure or eliminate the disease (*ārogya*), and on the means of healing (*bhaiṣajya*).

The therapeutic system of yoga holds that one must overcome the tendency to be involved in and to identify with the processes of daily existence, since these processes involve suffering. The source of this suffering lies in the false connection one makes between the world of phenomena and the principle of awareness. The world of phenomena (*prakṛti*) includes both the external world and the inner phenomenal self, the individual, namely the "I" in its existential and mundane sense. The principle of awareness is beyond body and mind; it is the "real Self," or the "pure Self" (*puruṣa*). In other words, suffering stems from the confusion between these two principles and from not recognizing them for what they are.[9] The confusing connection between the true Self and the world of phenomena can be pulled apart by means of discerning insight or wisdom[10] in a manner that can lead to liberation.

While the healing method of yoga is similar to the healing method of the Buddha, it is important to recognize where they seem to be fundamentally different. According to yoga, the source of the problem lies in the confusing connection between the world of phenomena and the true Self, whereas Buddhism locates the problem in the infinite thirst or craving inherent to one's personality. However, this significant difference, with all of its implications, may reflect no more than two points of view on the same state of affairs; that is, where the Buddha spoke from a psychological perspective, Patañjali's words reflect a cognitive perspective.

The long-haired yogi approaches the window. The wind blows through his hair. He is wrapped within and is silent. In his eyes, a question is reflected: *Yes, the reason and the path are known, yet the involvement and identification with daily conditioned existence continues. How do we overcome this conflict and dismantle it?* But in his eyes, an answer is reflected as well: *A mind that understood how such a confusing perspective was constructed will also know how to deconstruct it.*

It is clear that the insight that discerns the imposed and fictitious interwoven connection between the world of phenomena and the real Self must be more than a collection of explanations describing such a state of affairs. Such explanations, however deep they may be, are only ink on paper. At the same time, they also attest to an actual attempt to shift the gaze from the world of objects to the interiority of mind, a first step toward preparing the ground for the rise of discerning insight.

Since the principle of awareness, being the true Self, permeates the human mind, the different states of mind are mistakenly perceived as attributed and belonging to this principle. If the intellect (*buddhi*) is in a state of peace, joy and reflection (*sattva*), it will seem that it is the true Self that is the happy, clear and peaceful one. If this peaceful quality is distorted by the arousal of another quality characterized by fervor and passion (*rajas*), the sense of serenity will be replaced by a craving for pleasure and certainty. This causes the misconception that it is the true Self who is craving for pleasure and certainty. In the same way, if one's mind is stagnant, lethargic and passive (*tamas*), then a misconception will arise that it is the true Self who is experiencing dissatisfaction or boredom. These are all states of mind that we attribute to our Self, but in reality there is no connection between such states of mind and the true Self. Nothing can be imposed on the true Self. "Intelligence of mind" (*buddhi*) is confused with the true Self, which is pure awareness and exists beyond the body and mind, whose energy is experienced as thoughts. This misconception is something we are born into; the confusing interwoven connection between the real Self and the world of phenomena—of which the mind is an integral part—already exists from the very beginning.

With the thought *I breathe*, the true Self is identified with the activity of the breath and with the person who actually breathes. Therefore, according to yogic principles, we must abandon that thought. We must relinquish the notion that there is an agent, a performer, an individual subject within whom arises a sensation that can be expressed by the statement "I am the doer, I am the performer—*I breathe*." There is only the action and the objects *as they are*. Such existential, deep misidentification lies deep within the personality. We take it as self-evident. For the yogi, this identification is a fundamental and profound misunderstanding, and it is the reason that existence is filled with suffering, sorrow and pain.

The long-haired silent yogi seems to be intoxicated with the deep serenity, not breathing; his breath is suspended, indicating his exaltation. He abides in a special kind of *kumbhaka* of the fourth type.

In his interpretation of *sūtra* 2.51, the fifteenth-century scholar and commentator Vijñānabhikṣu[11] names it *Kevala-Kumbhaka*: a suspended breathing by a skilled yogi which is held for long periods of time, regardless of where the breath (*prāṇa*) is to be directed, the beats that are to be counted when inhaling, exhaling or holding the breath, and the number of times the exercise is to be repeated.[12] In fact, this state of suspended breathing occurs abruptly, by itself, and in accordance with an intense meditative concentration (*samādhi*), enabling the dawn of discerning insight (*vivekakhyāti*) and supernatural powers.

A living and breathing abyss is gaping between the breathing individual and the long-haired silent and ecstatic one, and his breath is suspended.

The principle of awareness or the true Self (*puruṣa*) is like sunlight shining on a stained and faded mirror, which is analogous to the mind (*citta*). Although this light does not demonstrate any special preference, prejudice or bias toward skin color, gender or origins, the objects in front of the mirror are reflected in a distorted way, through the grime and worn areas of the mirror. Thus, the stained, faded areas of the mirror may stand for one's concepts, beliefs, judgments, psychological tendencies and patterns of behavior, whether conscious or unconscious, positive or negative, upon which the world of phenomena (*prakṛti*) is reflected in one's mind. Because we are so habituated to perceiving the world in this way, without complete clarity of mind we suffer. We are sure that the source of the light that fills our minds is the ego (*ahaṃkāra*), just as the mirror that reflects the light is mistaken for the source of light. Yoga in action draws attention to that mirror by focusing and polishing it.

The act of polishing the mirror represents the unfolding, continuous and stable understanding that the mirror's natural function is merely to reflect, while being empty of any object. This understanding frees the mind of mental processes and empties it of any content that an object may invoke. The mind then stabilizes and abides in an empty yet clear and natural state. In order to purify the mind of its contents, one may shift and direct one's gaze from the world of sense objects, such as buildings or ideas and the contents and reactions they evoke, to the root of the mind itself. This allows one to discern between the source of light, representing the true Self, and the mind that reflects it as a mirror.

The special status of discerning insight, as a clearing of the confusion between the real Self and the world of phenomena, demands that we once again dwell on the meaning of yoga as a union or unification. It is not exactly a union between the pure subject, the real Self, and the world of sense objects, or the union of the true Self as the principle of awareness and the body, but rather it starts with the realization of their radical difference. Understanding the separateness or duality of these two principles—of pure awareness and matter—resolves one's confusion and consequently alleviates one's suffering. Although radically different in terms of epistemology, the real Self is not divorced from the natural processes that take place within the world of phenomena, those processes that reflect the Self and sense objects as the different animate and inanimate forms of communication.

The notion of yoga as a union is clearly expressed in its ontology in the sense that *puruṣa* as a principle of pure awareness, or true Self, ineffable and unknowable even to itself, is realized by means of meditation that stills and empties the mind of its contents and mental processes. Then, the true Self dawns and goes back to abide in its true nature and unites with the aggregate, all-embracing Selfhood.[13]

The notion of yoga as a union manifests within the practice of yoga in which its peak is the state of *samādhi*—being absorbed in meditative concentration in which the object of meditation alone emerges in the mind, which is stripped of all other contents. When the object of meditation does not ignite mental processes of conceptualization or judgment, a union between the pure subject or mind and the object of meditation can occur. The mind, stilled of mental processes except for awareness of the object itself, reflects the object of meditation just as a clear, polished mirror reflects an object, whether the object is static or on the move. The surface of the mirror is unified with the object's reflection. Yet there is a higher form of *samādhi* which is objectless; that is, it does not depend on any object in order to establish itself. The mind then, emptied of all content, enables a union in the sense that the true Self becomes rooted in the all-encompassing aggregate Selfhood. *Samādhi* enables the rise of discerning insight and supernatural powers, and this state of mind is radically different from the state of the ordinary, discursive and mundane mind.

Many translations and commentaries of the *Yoga Sūtras* have been written throughout the ages by classical commentators such as Vyāsa (fifth century) to Vācaspati Miśra (ninth–tenth century) and Vijñānabhikṣu (fifteenth century), as well as modern ones such as Swami Vivekānanda (end of nineteenth century), yogi Āraṇya, Swāmi Hariharānanda (1869–1947), Georg Feuerstein (1947–2012), Rohit Mehta (1908–1995), T. S. Rukmani, Yohanan Grinshpon, Ian Whicher, Edwin Bryant and Daniel Raveh, to name merely a few. However, in this work I am interested in extending the boundaries of the *Yoga Sūtras*' own context further from its historical, philosophical or philological explanations, taking a hermeneutical approach by exploring meanings in the text. This is motivated by existential interests and approached from a contemporary cultural background. Being such a concise text, almost every verse requires decoding in order to reveal both its overt and covert meanings, rendering it an exploration of the text's unknown properties, which are waiting to be discovered.

Although specific issues concerning the text—such as dualism, metaphysics, philology of key terms, the history of the author and the text itself—have been previously explored, I am interested in thinking with the text and focusing on the theme of the theory and practice of the psychology of yoga as presented within the text towards an exercise in yoga psychotherapy, one that is faithful to the text in a manner that does not dilute its essential meanings and ideas. Specifically, I intend to explore the notion of concrete yogic psychological methods, such as "cultivating the opposite" (*pratipakṣa bhāvanā*), transforming it further to "imagining the opposite," a practice aimed at healing negative habitual tendencies.

With this focus, I join a contemporary group of researchers such as Christopher Chapple, Mikel Burley, Ana Laura Funes Maderey, Stephen Phillips, Arindam Chakrabarti, Stephanie Corigliano and the contemporary commentators mentioned earlier who approach the text in a thematic way, exploring notions of body, imagination, death, idealism, realism and science of meditation, themes that have yet to be explored in the academic literature on the *Yoga Sūtras*.[14]

The practice of cultivating the opposite is at the heart of yogic practice. When we come in contact with a sense object it evokes a mental process, such as labeling, desiring, judging or rejecting it.

This practice is mainly contemplative, a reflective inquiry into the interiority of things. Patañjali chooses to present this method precisely in the context of negative thoughts and behaviors that violate the fundamental yogic moral rules (*yamas*), which are associated with violence, theft, sexual promiscuity, lust and greed. Such thoughts and modes of conduct carry a psychological-emotional burden or charge that has the potential to lead to blindness and loss of control.

In *sūtra* 2.34, Patañjali goes on to describe the range of charged thoughts and emotions that could violate the *yamas* in relationship to their different intensities. Here is the *sūtra* of which the main theme is *pratipakṣa bhāvanā*, or cultivating the opposite:

> To cultivate the opposite is (to reflect upon the fact) that thoughts which contradict the *yama-s*, such as violent thoughts and so on, whether executed, planned to be executed, or even approved, whether driven by greed, anger, or delusion, whether mild, moderate, or intense, result in endless suffering (*duḥkha*) and ignorance (*ajñāna*).[15]

In other words, the cultivation of the opposite can be applied not only to the mental processes that preoccupy the mind, but also to the patterns of behavior, habitual tendencies or imprints of past events that are etched into one's mind and remain concealed and dormant, as they too may cause a person to act them out. The cultivation of the opposite lies at the heart of yogic practice, and it is also the heart of the psychological method that seeks to address emotional tensions that arise in the wake of negative thoughts about the potential violation of yogic ethics rules, and to resolve them.

Chapter 1 addresses the basic concept of Patañjali's psychological method and the therapeutic paradigm it offers. In Chapters 2 and 3 I discuss "the practice of the opposite," which is at the heart of the yogic method. One aspect of the practice is to trace the motives for the thoughts and behaviors that violate the principles of yogic morality, and to cultivate the opposite of these negative motives. Another aspect of the practice is to actually focus on the results of thought and behavior that violate the principles of the yogic ethic, a profound process that is generated by self-honesty, sensitivity to others, remorse, and the use of imagination (*bhāvanā*). This is a comprehensive and prolonged yoga practice, which touches upon a vast range of negative behavior patterns at several levels of intensity, from patterns that have already manifested themselves and have been acted out, to those that are currently manifesting themselves, or are about to be manifested.

This practice is a major milestone on the road map of yoga which traces various paths to liberation. This practice is based on the path of yoga that Patañjali outlines in his text, as well as on classical commentaries on his text, such as those of Vyāsa and Vijñānabhikṣu, and on contemporary ones, such as Dr. Georg Feuerstein (1947–2012), a German Indologist specializing in the philosophy and praxis of yoga, who wrote over thirty books on yoga, tantra and Hinduism, and Rohit Mehta (1908–1995), an Indian theosophist and social activist who worked with Mahātmā Gandhi. In this work, I will reexamine the practice of the opposite in an expanded interpretation in which I discuss the potential of the imagination to allow the yoga practitioner to overcome the causes of affliction.

However, this practice is difficult to implement and is lengthy, since the mental imprints are painful and often remain latent. Only when the afflictive mental imprints are blocked or pacified can the mind become peaceful for long periods, offering the practitioner increasing relief. But what will the yoga practitioner do until then with his stubborn habitual tendencies that repeatedly inflict pain and harm on himself and others? What will he do about his habitual tendencies that prevent him from moving toward personal growth and harmonious relationships with his family, friends and community, as well as the realization of yoga?

Chapter 4 addresses these questions and examines the contours of practicing the opposite as a psychological yogic method in the context of Western psychology. But this is not a comparative study. There is no attempt to integrate or merge these two methods, but rather to emphasize and clarify the main aspects of yoga's psychological methods. By means of a case study, I will show how a Western psychological approach can undo mental imprints or habitual tendencies, even compulsive ones, in an efficient and focused manner that may complement yoga practice. In other words, I will propose a reexamination of the psychological methods of yoga, including their classical, traditional and modern interpretations, and discuss their potential application within the framework of modern psychology.

Chapters 5 and 6 present the psychological methods that are part of Tibetan Buddhist yoga. The *Ati Yoga*, known mainly in the West as Dzogchen, is extensively expressed in the works of Longchenpa, the fourteenth-century Tibetan Buddhist teacher. To be more specific, Chapter 5 discusses Patañjali's yoga and Longchenpa's Dzogchen and their opposing approaches to liberation, philosophy and their practice. Both methods are considered here as yogas in their broadest sense: spiritual practices at the heart of the traditions of Hinduism, Buddhism and Jainism, aspiring toward liberation in the most inclusive manner. The differences between the two methods represent an intriguing contrast between a gradual, intensive Indian yoga practice and immediate, effortless Tibetan yoga of non-action, which is also expressed in the psychological methods of yoga and Dzogchen. Although I provide an overview of the differences between the two methods, my intention is not to compare them, but rather to examine (in Chapter 6) the methods of Dzogchen in order to deepen the yoga practitioner's understanding of the psychological method he adopts. The psychological methods of Dzogchen relate to the release of emotional and mental burdens, confined thoughts, and emotions that the practitioner was unaware of. These methods unsettle his habits, and with the release of the emotional and mental burden that has accumulated in his psyche, the practitioner is able to engage in contemplation that enables the realization of his natural mind.

While Chapter 4 considers the differences and complementarity of yoga and modern psychology, Chapter 6 examines the possibility of merging the two approaches: the non-dual awareness of the Dzogchen method and modern psychology. I will review how this integration may assist both the Dzogchen practitioner and the patient.

In the epilogue, the voice of the long-haired yogi returns, not as a voice detached from mundane reality, but rather a voice that emerges from it, sounding ever clearer as the yoga practitioner improves his capacity to overcome his habitual tendencies to violate the moral principles of yoga. This time it is Patañjali's own voice. He notes that, with the fulfillment of these principles, the yogi gains special powers. Vyāsa notes that violent behavior, on the other hand, leaves the offending person in the underworld, battered and bruised. Such a personal system of reward and punishment raises questions about the status of yoga ethics in relation to other texts, such as the Bhagavad Gītā, yogic-tantric texts or Western moral philosophy, which includes aspects of moral relativism, utilitarianism, moral egotism and others. These dynamic questions open up possibilities for future research that could shed light on the ethical principles of yoga and the ultimate vow (*mahā-vratam*), that, according to Patañjali, must be observed independently of place, time, circumstances, socioeconomic status or social status.

Finally, in a quest to fulfill the principles of yoga ethics, I will summarize the practice of the opposite and identify *vairāgya* as an uninvolved awareness, an essential component of practice. Yoga practitioners may be able to use these exercises, while at the same time they may turn to other methods in Western psychology as a complementary and temporary treatment of negative habitual tendencies. The same applies to religious followers who need treatment or who cause suffering to themselves and others while trying to apply the commandments and the moral principles of their religion.

1

The Psychological Layers in Patañjali's Yoga

The Building Blocks of the Psychological System

The key to realizing yoga practice, both as a release from conditioned existence and as a way of improving one's well-being, is the mind, the *citta*. The term *citta* originates in the Sanskrit root *cit*, meaning to identify, observe, perceive or illuminate. This concept is usually translated as the Western term "mind."[1] Although Patañjali, the third-century CE author of the authoritative text, the *Yoga Sūtras* (which outlines in 195 concise, condensed verses a deep psychological framework), does not directly define the concept of *citta*, one can infer from its context that it stands for the complex structure of all of the mental and physical functions of the mind.

Citta includes three main subsystems. The first is *manas*, which receives, translates and categorizes sensory data into concepts; the second, *asmitā*, is the sense of *I-am-ness*, the "phenomenal ego"—the ego or the existential, everyday personality that coordinates processes such as thought, desire, imagination and physical action; and finally, the *buddhi* is the seat of reason, discernment, intuitive wisdom and intelligence.[2] When one comes in contact with a sense object, such contact ignites in one series of mental processes such as judgment, labeling, aversion or attraction in relation to the object. Dynamic interactions or mental processes take place among these three subsystems.

For Patañjali, yoga is the stilling or quieting of the changing states of the mind.[3] He categorizes and defines these mental processes in *sūtras* 1.6 through 1.11. These include correct and valid knowledge (*pramāṇa*) derived from inference (*anumāna*), verbal or textual testimony (*āgama*), and from direct perception (*pratyakṣa*), as well as false knowledge (*viparyaya*), superimposed conceptualization (*vikalpa*), sleep (*nidrā*) and memory (*smṛti*). Almost all of the mental processes indicated here are essentially cognitive. The last two, sleep and memory, are more closely associated with the psychological dimension of yoga, which is the focus of this book.

Sleep, of course, lets us dream. Dreaming is a reworking of impressions absorbed throughout the day. They include the desires, fears, personality and circumstances of the dreamer. For certain schools of modern psychology, dream content is the raw material for the therapeutic process. Patañjali, however, is particularly interested in putting an end to dreaming. This is because dreaming itself is a mental activity, a process that must be shut down. Since analysis of dream content can perpetuate and proliferate mental activity, the residue of latent subliminal mental imprints will continue to accumulate in a manner that may cause suffering. Such a process has the potential for action, which in turn will continue to conceal the true Self. A person can believe in the messages presented in the dream, treat them obsessively, and follow and act them out instead of seeing dreams as they are: expressions of feelings, passions, aversions, fears, projections and wishes.

Here is an example of how subliminal mental imprints are related to dreaming. Tom, who had grown up in an unsupportive home, watched an event in a playground in which a parent expressed cold contempt for his child. That night Tom dreamed he had a similar interaction in which he sharply criticized his son for receiving unsatisfactory grades at school. He woke up with a feeling of dissatisfaction and alienation. When Tom sat down to breakfast with his family, his son responded to his mood. His spirit sank, deepening the cold distance between them.

The incident on the playground undoubtedly challenged Tom, whose childhood experiences had created the mental imprint that he was not good enough, with which he was continuing to identify. The fact that the mental imprint had remained subconscious helped Tom evade the pain of his childhood experiences; however, he was not able to escape it completely. Despite the passage of time, the feeling of not being good enough lingered on, and he transmitted this feeling to his son, projecting it onto their relationship. Moreover, the withdrawal, distrust and distance the son felt for his father may have also challenged Tom, thus locking them into a vicious cycle.

The residue of subliminal imprints requires specific circumstances in order to manifest and be expressed. In this sense they are like seeds, which need the right amount of soil, light and water in order to germinate. Most dreams derive from subliminal imprints. Their content is awakened and expressed in dreaming, through their interpretation and according to one's subjective narrative. The dreamer is then captivated by the dream. The inability to recognize the dream as a dream is a symptom of ignorance (*avidyā*). Ignorance is in fact a misconception, a distortion or a confusion between actual reality and its subjective interpretation, which is capable of perpetuating painful experiences such as the one between Tom and his son. Identifying the dream as a dream means understanding that it is but a mental activity that, according to Patañjali, must be brought to a halt. Patañjali suggests that states of sleeping and dreaming may be taken as objects for the establishment of steadfast meditation. Then the mind is in a state of concentration, aware of dreaming and sleep states, and it becomes more and more stable without being trapped or caught up in dream content or heavy sleep.[4] Nevertheless, it seems that Patañjali does not offer a detailed or direct yoga practice that is capable of undoing the dreamer's identification with the dream and stilling the mind's activity when asleep. Yoga dream practice, which develops the awareness or the recognition that one is dreaming, appears in some of the Tibetan Buddhist traditions, such as Dzogchen. This training emphasizes the importance of using sleep for practice. Practice begins with a meditation focused on a particular object before bedtime. Gradually, the concentration loosens and its intensity diminishes, and the mind remains steady and in control, integrating this relaxed state of concentration with sleep. It enables the dreamer to recognize his dream as such, and then to discern between his intrinsic, pure awareness (*rigpa*) and the contents of the dream, and at times even to gain control over it.[5]

According to Patañjali, the dream is a mental activity that has to be shut down, a claim that corresponds to his definition of yoga as the cessation of mental activity.[6] Hence, one can assume that dreamless sleep is consistent with the purpose of yoga, because it seems emptied of mental activity. But sleep without dreams may also occur when the *tamas*, one of the three qualities (*guṇas*) that characterize the world of phenomena, experiences and events, becomes dominant over the other two. *Tamas* means "darkness," a term that describes stagnation, passivity, lethargy or heavy fatigue. In such mental states, the sleeping person is not at all aware of dreaming. He may awaken from such a dreamless sleep experiencing pain, confusion or joy for no apparent reason. These residues clearly indicate previous mental activity, even though the dreamer does not remember the contents of the dream.

The Sāṅkhya,[7] one of the six schools of Hindu philosophy, seeks to describe the dynamics of existence and the array of forces that operate within the world of phenomena that influence man. It examines these forces according to the display of the three *guṇas*, or qualities. *Sattva* is purity, clarity, serenity and neutrality. *Rajas* is dynamism, passion and craving, and *tamas* is stasis, heaviness and lethargy. These three qualities constantly interact with one another. At any given time, one quality will dominate over the other two, like a triangle whose shape is constantly changing. When one of its sides grows longer, the others become shorter, and the angles become more and more acute.

The dominant *guṇa* in yoga—both as a means and as a goal—is, of course, the *sattva*. Since it is the desired *guṇa*, one must attain its purest state, which is based in the *buddhi*, the seat of reason, discernment, intuitive wisdom and intelligence. Then the *buddhi* is purified and emptied even from the insightful wisdom that has accumulated over time.

Patañjali is not interested in the content of dreams, except perhaps for the dream as omen (*ariṣṭa*).[8] Omens can provide an early warning of the imminent death of the dreamer, or of another person.[9] Such information can be obtained from meditation on karma as the principle that one's actions determine one's current existential conditions, exactly in the same way one's current actions determine one's future, or from signs and symbols. It signals to the yoga practitioner that he must take advantage of the time left by eliminating distraction from his life and focusing on yoga. Such omens can appear in dreams that arise from the relatively deep and pure layers of the *buddhi*, woven from positive latent mental imprints that provide clarity. Although dreams are but a mental activity that must be brought to a halt, omens that appear in dreams can be temporarily useful for the practitioner enhancing clarity. Usually the dreamer remembers his dream vividly, and its information appears in great detail. According to the great Dzogchen master Chögyal Namkhai Norbu Rinpoche (1938–2018),[10] such a dream mostly occurs around dawn, just before waking, when the dreamer is relaxed and his sleep becomes lighter. The information that is revealed in a dream is like a ray of sunlight that shines through the clouds on a winter day. It represents the heightened clarity and calmness that are the result of yoga practice.

Memory (*smṛti*) is another category of mental activity that must come to an end. Of course, this category contains a vast range of experiences, possibly based on formative events or trauma, and they can determine the way we think and behave. Memory is presented as a mental process of fluctuation (*vṛtti*) that must be restrained and stilled. It provides continuity to an experience in one's past, even though the event has ceased to exist. Long after the event is over, the experience associated with it may remain unresolved and incomplete, leaving a conscious or unconscious desire to undo the painful imprints etched in one's mind. Due to the innate desire for release, painful memories associated with past events and experiences may surface repeatedly. Each time they reoccur, one has the opportunity to choose to undo them.

Generally speaking, human existence is driven by the desire for certainty, pleasure, safety and delight, as well as for the eternal. Such cravings preoccupy the mind and generate mental processes that constantly attempt to recreate the positive experiences associated with objects and events from the past. When these desires are not satisfied, negative emotions, such as anxiety, hostility, jealousy and anger, may prevail. Yet, when these desires are satisfied, one will attempt to hold on to them in order to extend the satisfying experiences and replicate them over and over, while at the same time fearing their loss.

According to Patañjali, yoga is fully realized when memory is stilled and restrained. For him, memory refers to concrete objects in a waking state and to intangible objects in a dream state.[11] One's personality or individuality is formed from a continuum of memories from childhood (and from previous incarnations) to the present day. Memory shapes identity. To restrain memory, therefore, would seem to erase one's subjective identity, making it a deeply counterintuitive act.

If that is the case, how are we to understand the state of amnesia, a situation in which the ability to remember is impaired? On the one hand, memory is one of the mental processes that Patañjali requires to cease in order to realize yoga. At the same time, it is clear that one who has lost the ability to remember is not necessarily free from the daily chains of the ego, nor from ignorance and suffering. As mentioned earlier, memory loss can occur when the quality of *tamas* (stagnation and mental heaviness) becomes dominant. But this kind of diminished or absent mental activity is not the restraint of mental activity that Patañjali was aiming for. On the other hand, memory is indispensable for existence—we cannot function without it. In fact, Patañjali himself wrote the *sūtras* employing letters and words to express ideas and meanings retrieved from memory. The activity of writing itself relied on memory, the muscle memory of the moving hand and fingers. Does this notion of memory contradict the yogi's desire to disengage from the world of phenomena? Is it an obstacle to cultivating a mind emptied of all content on the way to abide in the naturally aware, authentic Self?

It seems that we must reexamine Patañjali's requirement to restrain the memory in order to enable the yogi to disengage from the world of phenomena. In that case, it is possible to consider the notion of stilling mental processes as the yogi's highly evolved capacity to assert such stillness and to abide in it in different states of mind. Such a capacity for restraint may promote understanding that is driven by choice, not by the distorted or compulsive responses to past memories. In this way, memory is used appropriately; it is retrieved from a lucid mind in response to day-to-day necessities, circumstances or creative purposes. One can decide when to stop the flood of memories and when to stop activating mental processes. But, given that Patañjali's definition of yoga is the cessation (*nirodha*) of mental activity, one might ask if the yogi's capacity to bring his mind to stillness—alternating between abiding in imperturbable silence and breaking from it at will in order to guide people to liberation—is but another act that Patañjali teaches us to bring to an end.

Some researchers, such as Israeli Indologist Yohannan Grinshpon, consider yoga a method for the total separation of the true Self from the world of phenomena.[12] This separation leaves no trace of subliminal imprints and leads to an isolated, bodiless and memoryless liberation. That is, it is like the final liberation reached at the moment of death. Others, such as Canadian Indologist Ian Whicher, see yoga as an integration of the real Self with the world of phenomena, a merger that translates into engagement that brings with it far-reaching transformations in human nature, and to a liberated-present Self.[13] According to this approach, memory has its own place.

Israeli Indologist Daniel Raveh argues in his analysis of the great Indian philosopher Daya Krishna (1924–2007) that the composition of the *Yoga Sūtras* (the third-century text of 195 Sanskrit aphorisms on the theory and practice of yoga as guidelines or instructions [*anuśāsana*]), represents in itself a return to the world of phenomena from the isolated, bodiless and memoryless liberation in order to help people find their own way to liberation.[14] Separation or disengagement without such a return is effectively an attachment to another kind of separation. In other words, maintaining this extreme position is implicitly opposed to the idea of liberation. If so, separation and return, or engagement, are two components of yogic liberation. They both seem to exist at the same time in a vast and endless range of possibilities, perhaps even beyond the familiar world.

The yogi's most advanced ability to maintain the silence in its entirety and stay within its varied shades of states of mind represents for me a true quality of freedom: inhabiting a state of forgetfulness that allows for remembering. The ideas of the great Indian philosopher and speaker Jiddu Krishnamurti (1895–1986) about memory illustrate this very well. He agrees that memory is essential for us to function in everyday life,[15] yet he mentions that when he sees a beautiful cloud, a mountain peak touching the sky, or a face full of life and intelligence, he looks at them with great pleasure. He does not experience himself looking; he sees only the presence of beauty and love. At this moment, he, a viewer with no anxiety or distress, forgets what he saw and the emotions associated with it. If we were to ask Krishnamurti to describe to us from memory what he saw, he would certainly tell us about the sights and the pleasure he felt, but he would do so without the influence of psychological memory. Psychological memory is driven by the desire to recreate feelings of pleasure, because human beings are attached to and seek pleasurable experiences. Krishnamurti would use his memory not only to elicit and describe the sights he saw, but also to elicit the cultural context of the sights and linguistic skills required to describe them to us.

My mind returns to the long-haired yogi. Intoxicated by stillness,[16] long-hair does not remember, but also does not forget to tell us mortal human beings of riding the wind, and that his body can only be seen, not his innate, concealed and wonderful powers.

Although Patañjali points to the deactivation of memory, he identifies its positive but temporary function: the recollection of the elements necessary to establish a state of awareness, such as concentration or meditation inspired by a given object, whether external or internal. In *sūtra* 1.20, Patañjali writes: "Others reach that condition [of objectless Samādhi] preceded by faith, power, intentness [*smṛti*], concentration and wisdom." In general, the literal translation of *smṛti* is "memory," whereas here within the context of the present *sūtra* the translation is awareness, attentiveness or intentness[17] to indicate the mental process of stretching the mind toward an object and holding it in one's memory. The close connection between memory and attention is clear, as often the ability to remember information, names, people, events and experiences is directly related to the attention we devote to them.

Attention, however, also means the stretching of the mind toward an inner object; that is, one can direct attention inward to the memory storehouse and retrieve images of the objects required for the establishment of meditation. A skilled yogi can recall a picture of an object—for example, a rose, a mandala or the Shiva deity—and behold it in his mind. He can meditate at the sight of the picture, paying full attention to its components and details, its shape and color, until it occupies his mind entirely for a long time without distractions. Such practice can significantly stabilize the meditation and it will later enable the rise of yogic discerning insight.

Psychologically, the skillful inward redirection of attention may also consciously and unintentionally resurface painful experiences from the past. These experiences may affect one's present existence and impede the development of yoga and meditation practice. The yogi can identify these experiences and defuse their emotional charge. Painful experiences from the past may evoke emotions during an event in the present, such as fear of being alone, depression, or a feeling of meaninglessness. It is interesting to note that identifying these events, recalling them and experiencing them again through acceptance, without judgment and without defense mechanisms, can free the individual from their painful power.[18]

Thus, it can be concluded that memory, which plays a central role in improving attention and its application, aids in the practices of meditation and contemplation, while at the same time contributing to the relief of mental and emotional obstacles. Achieving the goal of yoga, the complete separation or isolation of the yogi from the world of phenomena, requires full control of memory, and this is made possible by the yogi's ability to maintain silence or stillness and stay within it. Then the true Self is revealed and self-awareness is fully present, untainted by mental processes.

As mental processes, sleep and memory are closely tied to subliminal imprints fixed in the mind. These connections continue to exist until the real Self separates from the world of daily phenomena. Until then, the problematic nature of these subliminal imprints will continue to arise. Sometimes even the possibility that these mental imprints will be exposed may trigger actions that accumulate karma, just like the metaphoric seed that can sprout only in certain conditions. And so, we return to our earlier question: What should a practitioner of Yoga, who is exposed to the many challenges of varying intensities contained within the subliminal imprints of mind, do about his habitual tendencies? What and how does Patañjali propose to resolve them?

Five *Kleśas*

To answer these questions, we need to examine another layer of the mind, which is made up of the five *kleśas*. These are the five causes of affliction that bind individuals to their sense of identity. They solidify the existential, ordinary, mundane self, and lock individuals into a vicious cycle of suffering.

If the mental processes mentioned in *sūtra* 1.5 are primarily concerned with cognition and perception of objects in waking and sleeping states, the causes of affliction are the five main forms of psychological reaction to the world of objects and events. The five causes of affliction referred to in *sūtra* 2.3 are: partial and relative knowledge based on false identifications (*avidyā*); the sense of self as solid personality, the phenomenal self (*asmitā*); attraction or acceptance (*rāga*); aversion or rejection (*dveṣa*); and fear of death (*abhinivesha*). In *sūtra* 2.2, Patañjali notes that it is possible to minimize the causes of affliction and thereby assist the aspirant on his path to liberation.[19] What, then, makes our psychological reaction to the world of objects and events into the source of affliction?

I'll start with the first *kleśa*, *avidyā*. This is the absence of Self-awareness that is perhaps not complete ignorance but distorted knowledge,[20] which stems from the inability to discern between the principle of awareness and the world of phenomena, which includes man and his physical, psychological and mental constituents. The state of *avidyā* conceals the principle of pure awareness and covers it by establishing a false identity, the sense of the ego. In *sūtra* 2.5, it is said that *avidyā* is mistaken identification, that it refers to the temporal as eternal, to the contaminated as pure, to sorrow as joy, and the ego as the true Self.[21] Such error of identification causes a person to perceive the existential-phenomenal self as the true Self. As we have seen, the way out of this deceptive error is the yogic insight or discerning wisdom (*Viveka-khyāti*).

Avidyā has psychological consequences for the four other causes of affliction to the extent that even experiences of joy and pleasure can be misleading, since they are also bound up in suffering. Pleasure means attachment to pleasurable objects. Attachment leads to action aimed at replicating that sense of pleasure. Karma is then created and becomes the basis for the next action, which will be triggered when the desire for the pleasing objects of desire and events resurface. Satisfying this desire will create karma that will be the basis for the next action, seeking and replicating the desired sense of pleasure. Such repetition of actions and reactions locks the person in a vicious cycle. For the discerning yogi, existence in *avidyā* involves pain and sorrow.

Consider: A person is sleeping at night, dreaming a nightmare and reacting with fear and anxiety. A cold sweat covers their skin. After they have lasted for a certain time in the grip of the nightmare, its intensity and density start to decrease, and the person realizes to their relief that it was only a dream. They then wake up as this actual insight liberates them from the painful grasp of the dream.

The inability to recognize the dream as a dream is a product of ignorance (*avidyā*), a misconception of actual reality perceived through subjective interpretation that creates a mentality of its own to which we are born, capable of perpetuating painful experiences. According to the metaphor, because of the inability to recognize the dream as a dream—or rather, because of the mistaken perception of the dream as reality—the dreamer unconsciously experiences a painful experience in which he is gripped with anxiety and fear. By identifying the dream as a dream, the yogi is able to distinguish intelligently between the dream and the principle of awareness, and between the ordinary self and the real Self. He realizes at once that this is only a dream, and experiences a profound insight that frees him from the false perception of the dream as a concrete reality, along with the anxiety it caused.

Despite the insight that it is only a dream, the yogi's initial reactions of fear, anxiety and the cold sweat caused by the nightmare remain etched in his mind. In other words, he will carry these emotions as subliminal imprints (*saṃskāras*), and in order to realize yoga, he will have to empty his mind of them as well. Hence, the next step on the journey of the yogi is the refinement of the discerning wisdom, so that it will rise immediately and spontaneously upon dreaming, while neutralizing the power of the *saṃskāras*.

The next cause of affliction is the sense of ego: *asmitā*. According to Patañjali, this feeling crystallizes as the seer becomes more and more identified with the apparatus of seeing. Hence, the sense of self or personality is nothing but the product of this mistaken identification between the one who sees and the apparatus of seeing. Here, the seer, according to Patañjali, is synonymous with the true Self, the *puruṣa*, the primal presence of awareness, otherness, which is neither objective nor subjective, whereas the power of seeing is erroneously attributed to the mind as its dynamic apparatus of perception is an integral part of the world of phenomena, *prakṛti*.

But it is only the inherent principle of awareness or the true Self (*puruṣa*) that provides one with the power of perception. The sense of self simultaneously arises as an inseparable part of the mind which is certain that it is not only a device of dynamic perception, but also the source of initial awareness (*puruṣa*) which enables seeing. Seeing them as one indistinguishable unit produces *asmitā*—the sense of ego.

The sun, the source of light, is used as a metaphor for the source of awareness, the One who sees. The mind is compared to a mirror and is associated with the sense of the ego, and the ability of seeing. Sunlight shines on a mirror, and from the mirror light is projected onto the objects in front of it, while the objects are reflected in the mirror. Similarly, the initial awareness of the true Self shines in the mind and provides it with the power of perception. However, the mind is convinced that it is not only a device of reflection and perception, but also the source of initial awareness, while in fact it is only reflecting, like a stained and worn mirror.

This constant confusion is so deeply embedded in the psyche that intellectual understanding alone is not enough to disentangle us from its tight grip. This is because the daily existential sense of I-am-ness (*asmitā*), responsible for intellectual processes, is itself made of concepts and thoughts. In other words, we can find ourselves in an almost impossible situation where the confused and entangled mind seeks to be released from the state with which it is identified, which is at its core the sense of the ego. Nevertheless, the deep understanding that the source of primordial awareness and the mind are not one indistinguishable unit but two fundamentally separate units is the key to resolving this confusion, for the mind is then directed at itself, and toward attempts to identify this confusion.

Most contemporary commentators believe that sense of I-am-ness is the ego, the empirical or phenomenal self that depends on the senses to perceive and cognize. The empirical or phenomenal self might even be considered an object in the process of self-reflection or inquiry. The ego, the bedrock of objective knowledge, actions and feelings, is intentional and constantly changing. When in contact with sense objects, tangible or intangible, the ego grasps and refers to them with a sense of identification and ownership. Everything the ego experiences is known to itself as its own—"my pleasure"—or something it identifies with—"I am angry." This sense of ownership or identification differentiates the individual as a unique being defined by personal boundaries.[22]

In Freud's view, the role of the ego is to reconcile instinctual impulses, desires and tendencies with the demands of morality and society. New Age commentators believe that the ego is about expressions of pride and excessive self-esteem or selfish conduct based on mistaken identity, and therefore its effect on the body and mind is negative. However, the sense of I-am-ness is not an enemy that should be avoided or repressed. Its function is temporary, and it is a positive and substantive one. Without it, it is impossible to build hospitals, develop productive agriculture, build homes, create art, educate values or alleviate the burden of human suffering.[23] The sense of I-am-ness is the most significant factor in one's decision to embark on the path of yoga and to search for liberation. After all, the real Self is already liberated, free even from the need for yoga as it abides in yoga from the very beginning.

At the same time, liberation means giving up the sense of I-am-ness, all that is known, both pleasant memories and painful experiences that have been accumulated and which have been etched in the ego. All this is in order to become acquainted with unfamiliar otherness, the real Self, that cannot be conceptualized but abided within. Such relinquishment has a profound psychological-emotional dimension. It is the horrific demand of yoga, a demand that can be learned from the words of Chögyam Trungpa, the Tibetan meditation teacher. In a documented oral dialogue, when asked by a student: "Why is it so hard to let go of one's ego?" Trungpa responded:

> People are afraid of the emptiness of space, or the absence of company, the absence of a shadow. It could be a terrifying experience to have no one to relate to, nothing to relate with. The idea of it can be extremely frightening, though not the real experience. It is generally a fear of space, a fear that we will not be able to anchor ourselves to any solid ground, that we will lose our identity as a fixed and solid and definite thing. This could be very threatening.[24]

Thus, according to Trungpa, the student has a primal fear of losing his identity and reference points. In order to emphasize the intensity and possible impact of the fear of absence, Trungpa repeats the notion of fear several times, using expressions such as "terrifying experience," "extremely frightening," "fear of space," "afraid of the emptiness," and "very threatening." At the same time, Trungpa also reassures the students by letting them know that in the real experience of emptiness one will not feel threatened or experience fear. Trungpa addresses the Buddhist notion of emptiness not only as the renunciation of the identity of the empirical self, but also as the renunciation of the true Self. Although the purpose of yoga, to abide within the real Self, is diametrically opposed to Buddhism, the merger with the real Self also threatens to strip the yogi of his empirical self, of the ego's sense of identity, and as such may also evoke the emotions associated with fear that Trungpa had spoken of that stem from the abandonment of identity.

The demand to give up his ego or sense of identity may confront the yogi with terror. According to the modern French philosopher Emmanuel Levinas (1906–1995), the initial response to coming face to face with the anonymous being, the "*il y a*" ("there is"), is the experience of horror. Levinas believes that *il y a* is independent existence; it is primordial and independent of the world of phenomena, and transcends both subjectivity and objectivity, interiority and exteriority. Although it is not a pure absence or nothingness, it cannot be perceived in discursive thought, for in *il y a*, discourse does not exist at all. It cannot be extinguished, it is anonymous and impersonal, and it pursues the identity of the ego in order to empty it of all that is personal. The *il y a* is the primary identity, the nucleus of the individual's Self, and precedes psychological and social aspects that shape the individual personality in relation to events and phenomena. When *il y a* invades the individual, it is impossible to escape; it is impossible to take shelter in facets of human identity or to retreat into that identity as if into a shell, because the invasion leaves the individual completely exposed and causes him to react with horror.[25] Levinas's notion of horror is not dissimilar to Trungpa's notion of fear of losing one's identity as a fixed, defined state.

The other causes of affliction (the *kleśas*), are the pairs of opposites: attraction and desire (*rāga*), or "moving toward," opposed to rejection and aversion (*dveṣa*), or "moving apart." In *sūtra* 2.7, Patañjali writes: "Attraction stems from a pleasant experience," and in *sūtra*

2.8, he added: "Rejection arises from a painful experience." It can be said simply that *rāga* is the desire for pleasurable events and objects of desire, and *dveṣa* is the avoidance or rejection of unfortunate events and objects that may cause suffering.

The inner movements of attraction and avoidance, which occur in the mind of the individual, are closely related to the events and objects of pleasure and pain stored in one's memory and the circumstances in which they have occurred. For example, pleasant memories of the past will impel one to replicate these moments of pleasure in present and future. We are attached to them, whether consciously or unconsciously, because of the hold the past has on us. Unconscious attachment is related to the dormant subliminal imprints and their emotional burden, and they have the potential to activate the phenomenal self, the ego, and motivate it to act out. Psychologically, the sense of the ego precedes attachments, for the "I" is the beneficiary or distressed one. The yogi transcends these two causes of affliction by freeing himself from their grip. Once he is no longer bound to them, they will not influence his actions.

Attraction and rejection as mental movements are expressed in varying intensities and emotional qualities. Attraction may range from relief to joy, caring to empathy, lust to sex. Rejection too may be expressed as a range of emotions, from restlessness to terror, lack of affection to loathing, irritation to rage. Even though Patañjali does not directly address the yogi's emotional world, his method touches on a wide range of emotions in all of their nuances—emotions which, of course, must be brought to cessation. It is this vast range of emotions that makes Patañjali's psychological method so significant. I will discuss this method in Chapter 2 through an examination of Patañjali's "cultivation of the opposite" and its therapeutic potential.

The categories of attraction and rejection are a pair of opposites. But what is the essence of their opposition? Take, for example, a situation in which we are driven by *dveṣa*, where we avoid facing the future out of fear of losing the present moment of pleasure, the object of our desire. Or a situation in which we are driven by *rāga*, where we quickly run away from painful circumstances in order to seek relief from the burden of pain. When desire for a particular object develops in the mind, it can generate at the same time a wish to reject the object of desire, and vice versa. For example, anger toward undesirable circumstances—*dveṣa*—also expresses longing for the desired state of affairs—*rāga*. For example, if we are on a diet, craving a favorite food such as chocolate also engenders the wish to avoid it. In certain circumstances, attraction and rejection may coexist as "mixed feelings," such as the mix of love and hate that a young person may feel toward high school, or a love that is accompanied by pain due to longing or dependence on a lover. In the experience of mixed feelings, a basic friction is created between the *kleśas*, and it is expressed as an internal conflict that produces pain and tension. Understanding the contrast between the *kleśa* of attraction and the *kleśa* of rejection has enormous significance; dismantling one *kleśa* of its emotional charge implies the dismantling of its opposite *kleśa*. This idea has potential implications for healing through Patañjali's psychological method of cultivation of the opposite.

And here we come to the last *kleśa*, the fear of death (*abhinivesha*). *Sūtra* 2.9 reads: "Clinging to life affects even the wise; it is an inherent tendency."[26] That is, even the wise have a basic instinct of self-preservation. Patañjali teaches us about wisdom using the Sanskrit root *vid*, which means "to know," hence the wise ones within the context of the *sūtra* are scholars. Their knowledge was acquired through a valid and correct means of knowledge derived from inference (*anumāna*), testimony (*āgama*) and direct perception (*pratyaksha*). These processes are mentioned in *sūtra* 1.7 as mental processes that should be brought to stillness. Thus, the wise ones will be equipped with the "right" knowledge, but their mind will still be preoccupied by subtle processes that should be brought to cessation. *Abhinivesha* is one of these mental processes.

The cessation of these processes also concerns the *kleśa* of the instinctive will to live, and it is contrary to our most intuitive self-perception. The contradiction between the desire to still the mind and the instinct to live teaches us about the temporality of things and events, including of life itself. What has come into being will also decay, and everything must be completely relinquished for the sake of Self-realization. Without a deep understanding of this truth of impermanence, life is characterized by an anxious search for certainty and caught up in a constant cycle of becoming, of change and decay. Life is bound up with the fear of death, which feeds the other causes of affliction: attachment, aversion, and the sense of I-am-ness.

Human beings have created psychological mechanisms that help them deal with the fear of death, such as denial—a mechanism that allows us to talk about the fear of death while dismissing it because "my time has not yet arrived"—or numbing the pain through intellectualization or black humor. These defense mechanisms have mental and physical expressions. Many of them are latent, as they are mental imprints that are stored in the mind. The fifth-century scholar and commentator Vyāsa believes that these imprints were created under the influence of death experiences of past incarnations; the fifteenth-century scholar and commentator Vijñānabhikṣu believes that they were created due to exposure to the death of others. But recurring dreams of death, such as falling into an abyss, may also leave their mark and intensify the fear. Although fear may be paralyzing, it may also spur one into a life of action and creativity. In any case, the mental imprint of the fear of death is etched in one's mind, and it is primal and natural in the sense that it has always been at the very core of life. In that sense it is thought to precede the other causes of affliction. According to Patañjali, Vyāsa and Vijñānabhikṣu, the fear of death is expressed conceptually; it is depicted as a cause of affliction through various interpretations and subtleties, but without directly describing its meaning, the emotional implications, or the defense mechanisms involved. Those are but mental processes that may once again lock one who fears death in the field that exists between *rāga*—clinging to life—and *dveṣa*, avoiding the fear of death.

Awakening and internalizing the discerning insight will indeed dismantle the fear of death and will lay bare the sense of I-am-ness, including its many core identifications, toward the real Self that is free from any identity. However, the fear is here. Present. What would happen then? And on what shore would I land? Clinging to ideas about the discerning insight, Self-realization, and the attempt to internalize it is a lofty but seductive possibility, and it entails denial of fear, of what is happening now. The inner gaze is turned toward the fear, follows it, observes it as its waves slowly retreat back into the ocean from which they rose. They are still echoing and their foam floats above the water.

The long-haired yogi is carried on the wings of spirit, outside his body, transcending it and revealing that only his body could be seen, and that he was not that body, alive or dead.

Patañjali continues to present to the reader the layers of a psychological framework, and in *sūtra* 2.4 he enumerates four states of the causes of affliction: dormant, weakened, suspended and active.[27] A dormant *kleśa* is covert, and may be activated in reaction to a particular stimulus. For example, a person leaves his house calm and relaxed and gets into his car. On his way he is snared in traffic and confronted by aggressive drivers. This arouses his own aggression and he begins to shout, insulting the drivers. That is to say, the person who seemed calm and peaceful as he was walking toward his car was actually already filled with dormant aggression that erupted in response to triggering circumstances.

A weakened *kleśa* is one that has been thinned by yoga practice, so that its ability to provoke the yogi into action becomes limited. For example, fostering a nonviolent attitude may gradually reduce involvement in violent verbal communication. But at the same time, when the suspended *kleśa* is temporarily suppressed, it may eventually come back into play. For example, a person may experience anger toward his employer, but he suppresses this feeling and instead shows kindness toward him. The anger, however, does not completely disappear. After a while it may manifest itself in a dream, for example, in which the person vents his anger on the employer. *Kleśa* in a waking state is active and escalating, like an emotionally charged argument that spirals from anger to rage, or from joy to intoxicating euphoria. Vyāsa also mentions a fifth state, in which the causes of affliction are completely weakened, emptied of their emotional charge. As such, they lose their power to cause one to react to triggering circumstances. They are like dry seeds that can no longer germinate.[28] This situation characterizes the yogi who is able to discern continually between the world of phenomena—in which circumstances may provoke action manifesting as the causes of affliction—and the real Self.

The *Saṃskāras*

The underlying psychology of the *kleśas* is a vast expanse of *saṃskāras*, dormant mental imprints that are etched in one's mind and remain concealed. These imprints have the potential to become active when triggered by external or internal stimuli, which may cause the mind to act. The action from these mental imprints is the karma.

In the *Bṛhadāraṇyaka Upaniṣad*, one of the early *Upaniṣads*, ancient Sanskrit texts of spiritual teaching and ideas of Hinduism, a description of the concept of karma is presented in the context of morality. Karma, according to this description, is what determines a causal and moral relation between action and consequence in a given social situation:

> What a man turns out to be depends on how he acts and on how he conducts himself. If his actions are good, he will turn into something good. If his actions are bad, he will turn into something bad. A man turns into something good by good action and into something bad by bad action.[29]

According to this principle, one's personal fate and all that transpires in one's life, family and social environment are the consequence of all of one's actions. There is no system of reward and punishment imposed on man by any divine entity, and there is no system that places the righteous and the wicked in tests of morality and faith. This means that one's current ethical or non-ethical actions are directly influenced by one's previous actions and their consequences, and these will also determine the quality of one's future actions. Thus, residue from actions, experiences and past events accumulate into mental imprints. The mental imprints are like undercurrents beneath the layers of mind, and they feed the *kleśas* when certain circumstances transpire that are the basis for the next actions. Their consequences will reproduce mental imprints, and these will activate and manifest through the five mental processes (*vṛttis*) previously mentioned, or as the causes of affliction. As noted, such mental processes or causes of affliction are preceded by mental imprints. The potential of mental imprints to spur action is based on an idea of causation that is conceived of a kind of circular process that has no apparent beginning.[30]

The *saṃskāras* are the hidden imprints in our unconscious, residue of our daily experiences—conscious and unconscious, internal and external, desirable and undesirable.[31] These imprints are assumed to be our basic self-perceptions, attitudes and beliefs that lie in the depths of our memory, and are composed of emotions, sensations and thoughts about past experiences or events.[32]

The mental imprints are interrelated, and collected and organized in configurations of imprints, attributes and tendencies. This configuration will depend on the intensity of the mental imprints and their respective weights in creating certain habitual tendencies, attitudes, thoughts, desires and images. Making a decision, for example, may seem to be a completely conscious process, but it is in fact influenced by mental imprints and the way they are organized. The formation of mental imprints is at the core of one's character, behavior and way of thinking. They are termed *vāsanās*.

The *vāsanās*, the tendencies of one's personality and imprints of thought and behavior, are related to the causes of affliction, the *kleśas*, as these affect human behavior. The intensity of each *kleśa*, its effect and the feelings it engenders in various circumstances, all shape the *vāsanās*. They are a collection of modes of behavior driven by rejection, attachment, fear of death, identification, and the emotions that are associated with them.

Vāsanās are expressed and manifest by means of the causes of affliction. For example, a person may develop a behavior pattern of submissiveness or obedience in order to avoid rejection and to feel a sense of belonging. The greater he fears social rejection, the greater will be his submissiveness and obedience. Raveh provides an accurate analogy that clarifies the connection between mental imprints and behavioral tendencies: the *saṃskāras* (the mental imprints) are like atoms, he notes, while the *vāsanās* (the behavioral tendencies) are like molecules. The *kleśa* is similar to a molecular unit. Like a mold, it dictates the shape, volume, intensity, expression and manifestation of any given tangible *vāsanā*.[33]

It is possible to understand the psychological themes embedded in the complex and intricate relationship of *saṃskāras*, the *vāsanā* and the *kleśas* through the character of Ebenezer Scrooge, the protagonist of

Charles Dickens's 1843 novel *A Christmas Carol*. The psychological profile of this character allows us to shed light on the psychology of yoga without getting caught up in the complex problems that arise when attempting to apply contemporary Western theories of psychoanalysis on the *Yoga Sūtras* of Patañjali, a text written in the third century.

Scrooge is a tough, greedy, rich man. His tightfistedness is described with exaggerated humor, a style very typical of Dickens. He describes the fire that warms Scrooge's office during the icy Christmas season, and he writes: "Scrooge had a very small fire, but the clerk's fire was so very much smaller that it looked like one coal. But he couldn't replenish it, for Scrooge kept the coal-box in his own room."[34]

Scrooge's miserliness was rooted in the poverty of his childhood. Young Scrooge had been neglected and abandoned. Following his mother's death, and shortly after the birth of his younger sister, his frightened, depressed father expelled him from the house. Lacking a stable, loving family, Scrooge became callous and cold. His early childhood experiences of rejection, loneliness, distrust and personal insecurity likely made him feel insignificant and unworthy of love. Out of stinginess, he rejected his nephew's invitation to Christmas dinner; he withdrew from human contact and warmth, refrained from giving presents, and refused to give charity. He had no compassion for the poor, and he believed that the world would be a better place without them. Stinginess and greed pervaded almost every aspect of his life.

These behaviors stem from the desire to experience control. Scrooge aspired to maintain the status of a rich, independent and powerful person in response to his formative childhood experiences of poverty and feelings of anxiety and helplessness. In the face of poverty, he developed a strong sense of self-preservation and identified with his wealth. Scrooge was blind to his own stinginess. He viewed his wealth as proof of his ability.

In general, the behavioral pattern of stinginess creates distress and impairs social functioning. It leads to an uncompromising demand for perfection and overemphasis on insignificant and meaningless details. It also leads to righteousness, toughness, stubbornness and, of course, to extreme caution in money matters along with difficulty separating from objects, even when they are clearly no longer used.

Scrooge's brief psychological description shows that the mental imprints etched in his mind relate to states of feelings or identity. The imprints are the totality of his inner attitudes and beliefs about himself and others. Emotions and identity are the result of memory-dependent feelings and are consequences of early childhood experiences of acute poverty. They are associated with difficult feelings of rejection, loneliness, abandonment, distrust and lack of physical security, as well as perceptions low self-worth and the sense that one is unworthy of love and appreciation. This residue was created by his early experiences and became etched in his mind. Together these *saṃskāras* formed a mental "molecule," and crystallized into a mental pattern: a personal characteristic, closely related to the imprints of thought and behavior. This is *vāsanā*, and for Scrooge it was expressed in his stinginess.

This tendency is reflected in the expressions of the *kleśas*, the causes of affliction: Scrooge's deep aversion (*dveṣa*) toward waste or resentment at parting from his money, or even from a single piece of coal; his greed and strong attraction (*rāga*) to situations that allow him to amass a fortune; his identity as a rich, arrogant businessman who knows the ways of the world (*asmitā*), despite his ignorance and lack of awareness of his stinginess and its implications; and finally, a strong sense of survival and self-preservation which is also a means of resisting the fear of death (*abhinivesha*).

Patañjali discerns between two types of *saṃskāras*:[35] the *vyutthāna* and the *nirodha saṃskāras*. The *vyutthāna* type forces the mind to direct the gaze outward at sensory objects, like a magnet attracted by metal objects. They perpetuate a distorted perception of objects and the sense of self. Such *saṃskāras* cause the pain and suffering that perpetuates conditioned existence. *Nirodha saṃskāras* intensify the control of mental processes and make them still. They enable the birth of an insight that discerns between the world of phenomena, the sense of the ego and the true Self.

When the *nirodha* type of *saṃskāras* block and still the *vyutthāna saṃskāras*, the mind becomes more peaceful. The more yoga is practiced, the more the layer of mental imprints of the *nirodha saṃskāras* will grow and solidify. The mental processes will become more and more quiet, and the mind will be peaceful for longer periods of time.

A practitioner of yoga who persistently and systematically fosters the *nirodha* type of *saṃskāras* achieves not only the release of the mind from the grip of the *vyutthāna* type, but also the rise of the discerning insight and total concentration, and with it the dawn of Self-knowledge abiding in it.

Vyāsa believes that with the rise of discerning wisdom that results from the total concentration of mind, new mental imprints are created. They delay and block the field of dormant mental imprints that underlie the existence of the world of phenomena, so that perceptions and beliefs arising from this existence no longer resurface. In other words, with the stillness of the mental processes dawns total concentration, the *samādhi*, and with it, the clear discerning wisdom, the *nirodha saṃskāras*, gather and proliferate. They obstruct the causes of affliction so that they can no longer take over the mind.[36] He notes that until the discerning insight arises, it takes a great deal of time and effort to create mental imprints of the *nirodha* type.[37] In essence, yogic meditation, the production of *nirodha saṃskāras*, is a powerful means of improving the ability to overcome the mental imprints that underlie the causes of affliction.

Despite the seemingly orderly presentation of the two types of *saṃskāras*, their behavior is not fully understood, since their mechanisms are not made sufficiently clear. Indian scholar and yogi Swāmi Āraṇya Hariharānanda (1869–1947)[38] and Indian Sanskrit authority T. S. Rukmani[39] claim that the *nirodha saṃskāras* are opposed to the *vyutthāna saṃskāras*. Feuerstein argues that *nirodha saṃskāras* obstruct or block *vyutthāna saṃskāras*;[40] Grinshpon maintains that they erase them;[41]Indian Scholar and yoga practitioner Pandit Usharbudh Arya argues that they interfere, nullify and inhibit them;[42] and Whicher claims they replace them,[43] while Indian yogi and writer Ramamurti Mishra (1923–1993) claims they destroy them.

In his commentary on the first *sūtra*, Vyāsa insists on the idea of two states of mind. He argues that a state of mind of one-pointed concentration (*ekagrata*) cannot destroy or eliminate *vyutthāna saṃskāras*. After this state of concentration ceases to exist, distractions begin to emerge due to exposure to the stimuli of sense objects, and they inhibit the accumulation of mental imprints of peace and wisdom, the *nirodha saṃskāras*. If so, as long as the mind is not free of distraction and does not develop a single, one-point concentration, the exposure of *vyutthāna saṃskāras* to various stimuli may affect the imprints of behavior and thought. Moreover, even in one-pointed meditation, when insight arises regarding a particular problem or difficulty, most of the time this insight can only temporarily resolve or release them. *Nirodha saṃskāras* do not necessarily annihilate or erase *vyutthāna saṃskāras.*

Thus, until the final liberation from bondage of ignorance, the *saṃskāras*, which bear the potential of suffering, are not resolved and are not in a state of inaction. But at the same time, they are still under the influence of a stronger force, the power of the *saṃskāras*, which have the potential to silence or still the mind. This potential is a continually renewing force; as the practice of yogic meditation progresses and intensifies, the practitioner accumulates more *saṃskāras* conducive to stilling the mind, and is more successful at blocking the *saṃskāras* that bear the potential of suffering, and he refrains from acting under their influence. It can be concluded that when the yogic practice is paused or stopped, the *saṃskāras* that bear the potential of suffering remain exposed, and under certain circumstances they will continue to dictate thoughts and actions that involve the causes of affliction.

If so, there seems to be some unspecified period in which the *saṃskāras* that bear the potential of suffering remain exposed. This condition raises the following question: How will the yoga practitioner manage his life under the influence of these mental imprints until such time that he is able to reach discerning insight? Is he condemned until then to fight them, to cause himself and others pain or harm, or to simply rely on the future promise that the power of stillness will increase? And what if mental imprints have long since crystallized into a pattern of deep, compulsive and repetitive behaviors that cause the practitioner to inflict existential harm and pain on his immediate environment?

These questions are also relevant to the causes of affliction, *kleśas*, because both the *vyutthāna* and *nirodha* types of *saṃskāras* correspond to two types of *kleśas*: those that inflict pain and suffering, *kliṣṭa*, and those that do not cause pain and suffering, *akliṣṭa*. As Feuerstein observes,[44] *akliṣṭa* refers to those events and mental processes that support yoga practice. In this way they deconstruct the *kleśas* of the *kliṣṭa* type that cause suffering. In other words, certain mental processes are considered effective when they are able to facilitate the resolution of other processes and to eliminate the mental activity involved with the causes of affliction. For example, an object-oriented meditation practice is based on fixing the gaze on an object such as a statue. It is the power of such meditation to delay or obstruct all distracting mental activity, except that which is associated with the practitioner's gaze. The practitioner's gaze is also motivated by the intention driven by the sense of I-am-ness, the *asmitā*, for even the very choice of the specific object of the meditation object can be driven by a profound and deep attraction, namely *rāga*.

Feuerstein further explains that the yogi who confronts one type of mental imprint with the other, without allowing these imprints to take on a mental form of thought that leads to action, will indirectly cancel and obfuscate both types of imprints. The process in which one cause of affliction blocks another cause of affliction is compared to a pair of millstones that continue their grinding even after the grain has been milled, causing both stones to disintegrate.[45] The metaphor is not entirely accurate, at least not in the short term, since it does not deal with the emotional tension that may arise out of the disparity between one's aspirations and the actual situation. Consider, for example, meditation that is motivated by the desire for a sense of peace but performed in times of anxiety, or the attempt to avoid anger by practicing compassion. In such situations, an inner conflict is created by two opposing subconscious emotions, and in certain circumstances this conflict can bring us to action.

The central question remains: How can yoga help a person acting under the influence of mental imprints? After all, these imprints have long since crystallized into a deep, compulsive and repetitive behavioral pattern that may inflict pain. Will he have to deal with acute behavioral tendencies until he gains discerning insight? Is he condemned to battle them while inflicting suffering on himself and his surroundings? After all, the process of shutting down the deep mental imprints that potentially cause suffering may be a prolonged one. How then can one release the emotional burden; that is, the mental imprints and their related causes of affliction? What psychological method does Patañjali propose to help dismantle the emotionally blinding burden that fixates a person in *avidyā*?

The long-haired yogi is silent. He had already left these questions.

2

Pratipakṣa Bhāvanā
Cultivating the Opposite

The contradictory forces of both types of *saṃskāras* are active in the subconscious, and each one works to subjugate the other. The latent *saṃskāras* of pain and suffering are not disabled nor uprooted, but are dependent on a greater force, which is continually renewed by the consistent and repetitive practice of meditation. This brings us back to the methods that Patañjali proposes to intensify the mental imprints produced by stillness. These can be indirect or direct. Each gives the yoga practitioner access to his subconscious mental imprints in order to erode or dissolve them. Indirect methods give practitioners gradual control or restraint over thought, behavior and action, all aspects that are affected or dictated by mental imprints. Direct methods, on the other hand, may provide direct access to the mental imprints themselves in order to heighten awareness so as to undo their conditioning force and their emotional burden.

Pratiprasava and *dhyāna* are indirect methods. *Pratiprasava* changes the direction of one's gaze and shifts it from the world of objects and mental processes associated with them in one's mind toward the mind itself. One then aims toward a gradual composure that is refined over time. This composure reaches its peak when the phenomenal mind dissolves into its origins, into the base of the world of phenomena (*prakṛti*) from which the mind is inseparable. Usually one's mind is directed outward to the realm of objects, or inward to one's psychological world. In both cases, the mind usually reacts to a stimulus, conditioned by particular circumstances. However, when the yogi realizes complete stillness after the mental imprints have dried up and lost their agency, his mind returns to the source of the world of phenomena.

Dhyāna is a meditation in which the mind focuses on one object and becomes silent. Only the train of thoughts associated with the object of meditation remain. As meditation matures, it develops into a remarkable, intense concentration that brings with it clarity and wisdom. The method of *Pratipakṣa bhāvanā* is the simultaneous implementation of *pratiprasava*, the shift of one's gaze to one's interiority of mind, and of *dhyāna*, meditation. *Pratipakṣa bhāvanā* means "meditation on the opposite," or "cultivation of the opposite." The cultivation of the opposite is a fundamental and practical principle in the yogic program. It can be seen in action in all eight limbs of Patañjali's yoga. Yoga essentially changes the meanings we attribute to conventional life, because according to yoga doctrine, complete stillness of mind and liberation are values that are more important than conventional social values associated with money, sex and power. Liberation, according to yogic principles, is freedom from the compulsiveness involved in sustaining conventional day-to-day values; that is, liberation from the phenomenal ego and the personality that reconstructs and solidifies itself and its mental and material environment.

Pratipakṣa bhāvanā is more than a specific self-remembering of the moral principles of goodness in a situation in which they are about to be violated. Its essence is a long and strenuous meditative process in which one's internal gaze identifies a cause of affliction and cultivates its opposite. It refers not only to cultivating the opposite, practicing the opposite, or meditating on the opposite, but also to *imagining* the opposite.

Patañjali's direct method proposes to dismantle the subliminal imprints and empty them of their potential for action when they are meditated upon. Such deactivation of mental imprints is made possible through immediate, direct insight, unmediated by any verbal conceptions, elaborate explanations or value judgments. This insight enables one to become immediately aware of a particular event that has left its mark on one's mind. Mental imprints involve a subjective reaction to a particular past event. For example, intense anxiety may form in reaction to a past event that created a subliminal mental imprint, or *saṃskāra*: "I am not safe." This *saṃskāra* was produced in response to a threat. It continues to occupy one from the moment of the past event and dictates one's life situations and conditions. The insight that identifies the *saṃskāra* directly is not analytical or intellectual, but bypasses the intellect and arises in one intuitive and immediate moment of wisdom. It frees the yogi from the grasp of the *saṃskāra*. In our example, it frees him from the sense of threat that was etched in his mind.

The next chapter will further address the direct methods of emptying mental imprints of their content and their conditioning force. Let us first review the indirect methods.

Pratiprasava, or Concentrating on the Opposite

As mentioned in Sūtra 4.34, when the *guṇas* return to their source, the power of the pure and empty mind also returns to its natural state. In this state, the real Self is isolated from the material world of phenomena and from the inner mental-psychological world and presents itself as aloof.[1] Here the term *pratiprasava* refers to a movement of convergence toward the source of the mind rather than a movement of degeneration or disintegration. The *guṇas*, the three qualities that characterize activity in the phenomenal world, cease and dissolve into their source. They are then in a state of a perfect static equilibrium in which they nullify one another. Then the true Self, the principle of pure awareness, is liberated from the confusing entanglement with the world of phenomena characterized by the constantly vibrating or stirring forces of the *guṇas*. Mental processes are an inseparable part of the world of phenomena, and when the true Self is liberated from the mistaken identification with them it remains in its natural state. By definition, this state is free and pure awareness.

As shown in Sūtra 2.10, *pratiprasava* has an important psychological role: "In their subtle form, [the *kleśas*] can be overcome by involution [*pratiprasava*]."[2] That is, the causes of affliction have their roots in the mind, which are concealed habitual tendencies that can be overcome by applying the method of *pratiprasava*. Overcoming them means relinquishing the tendency of the mind to objectify the phenomenal world and focus on its origin, becoming still. Vyāsa[3] adds that it is because of *pratiprasava* that the causes of affliction lose their compelling power and ability to produce mental processes. He illustrates this deactivation of power with the metaphor of a dry seed that has lost its potential to germinate. The final dissolution of the causes of affliction occurs only when the mind turns and converges into itself, imperturbable, still. So even the positive mental imprints that are necessary for the realization of yoga, such as the perception that the body is not the real Self, are dissolved and emptied of their content and power. Even this perception, a mental imprint that still indicates sense of ego, must be abandoned.[4]

A number of possible interpretations can be derived from the term *pratiprasava* based on its central meaning: a process of involution; that is, an inverse process of evolution in the sense of a return to origins. Involution does not refer to the movement toward degeneration, regression or decay. Nor does it refer to a small seed in which the entire plant is contained, innate and embedded, for according to Vyāsa's metaphor, such a seed will also dry up and lose its power to germinate.

One wave rises and recedes in the lake, then another wave rises and recedes until the moment that the lake becomes clear and still. So too are the mental processes that rise and recede back into the mind without prompting new ones, until the mind is lucid and still. This is yoga.

This interpretation of *pratiprasava* as a process of involution suggests that it is possible to delve into the roots of the causes of affliction, the hidden mental imprints, in order to empty them of their content. This process begs a series of psychological questions: Why do we desire a certain object, whether tangible or abstract, but reject another? What determines one's preferences? What motivates one to cling obsessively to the sense of the ego, I-am-ness, in order to confirm one's identity and existence vis-à-vis others?

Like a magnet that is attracted to metal, so too is the gaze directed at objects that can be grasped by the senses. *Pratiprasava* demands that the focus of attention be shifted. It seeks to establish an inner mental gaze through which to examine the causes of affliction and to ponder how they dictate one's interaction with people and the world of phenomena. Such an inner gaze helps to understand the effect of the causes of affliction and the manner in which they are manifest. It may also aid in identifying the key patterns of thought and behavior that characterize one's personality, and explain how one experiences the world of phenomena, its events and interactions, while revealing the blind spots that obscure mental clarity.

Mehta believes that *pratiprasava* is first and foremost an intellectual method. It allows us to identify the factors that motivate one to perpetuate conditioned existence and patterns of thinking and behaving caused by such existence.[5] Although he believes that intellectual understanding is necessary for the establishment of the inner gaze, understanding alone does not necessarily change these patterns of thinking and behaving, it is just the first step toward calming the mental processes. It is a signpost on the path to liberation, culminating in the aloofness of the real Self, isolated and released from the entanglement with the world of phenomena.

It is possible to expand the meaning of *pratiprasava* and perceive it not only as an intellectual process but also as a psychotherapeutic process of unraveling what has already been learned. In this process, the person's attention focuses on undoing their negative tendencies in order to weaken them, and instead enable openness. This process involves observing painful physical sensations and feelings. Here, one questions how these feelings and emotions are related to a specific problem or recurring tendencies that cause pain, and one tries to understand how over the years the hidden mental imprints have solidified into a set of self-perceptions, beliefs and values.

Thus, *pratiprasava* is also a method of psychological understanding, acquired by identifying one's dominant patterns of thinking and behaving and analyzing their causes. Identification is essential to another method which is also used to observe the compulsive patterns that are expressed through the causes of affliction. It is based on non-judgmental reflection, one of the main characteristics of meditation. Observing without distractions encourages mental clarity, through which hidden mental imprints and the causes of affliction are identified, reflected upon and dealt with. The principal method for enduring causes of affliction is presented in Sūtra 2.34, which centers on how to deal with modes of thought and behavior that concern the violation of basic moral rules (*yamas*). I will return to this point later in the discussion.

Dhyāna: Uniform, Stable and Continuous Concentration

Patañjali clearly notes that the mental processes resulting from the causes of affliction can be overcome through *dhyāna* (meditation), uniform, stable and continuous concentration on a certain object.[6] Clearly, the goal of meditation is to create a state of mind of imperturbably focused concentration that is not distracted by internal or external stimuli, thoughts or sensations. Such concentration is an object-oriented activity in which the mind becomes calm and stable, and mental and discursive processes are slowed down and pacified. As soon as thoughts or other content in the mind recede and subside, serenity and clarity emerge. In this state, the subconscious mental imprints that result from yoga and meditation practice are activated, causing stillness. Once such yogic subconscious imprints overpower those afflictive ones, their capacity to cause suffering will decrease and they will no longer dictate thoughts and behaviors.

Meditation can create a gap or a space between stimulus and reaction and cause and effect, for while a cause of affliction floats and resurfaces because of its recollection or because of its concrete occurrence, the mind is focused and able to observe it. This gap provides the space for a considered response instead of conditioned reaction to stimuli. When the practitioner of yoga is present in a one-point, continuous and resolute concentration, he is not conditioned by the causes of affliction or subject to its influences. In time, this concentration allows for the realization of the discerning insight which undoes the confusing tangled weave that binds the real Self to everything else. Under the influence of meditation, the link between the causes of affliction and their consequences is also broken. Repeated practice of meditation allows a practitioner to remain in a calm, abiding state of mind for longer durations, and to develop a discerning wisdom that becomes dominant in one's mind on the journey toward liberation.

Pratipakṣa Bhāvanā, or Meditation on the Opposite

The most effective application of *pratiprasava* and *dhyāna* is achieved in their integration; that is, the use of meditation to shift the direction of mental processes into stillness. This is the method of *pratipakṣa bhāvanā*, meaning "meditation on the opposite," or "cultivation of the opposite," which can create new, positive, subconscious mental imprints of restraint and silence. In Sūtra 2.33, Patañjali states that in order to stop thoughts of violating the moral principles of yoga, the practitioner must concentrate on their opposite.[7] This refers, for example, to the desire to cause physical or mental harm to others, or to steal their possessions. The yoga practitioner is guided to recall the moral opposite of such thoughts and apply them without rationalizing or justifying them. Nevertheless, the moral antithesis of such thoughts requires further examination.

According to the method *pratipakṣa bhāvanā*, applying the opposite does not mean that the practitioner will endeavor not to be angry in circumstances that cause anger. He is not required to be in a state in which anger is absent or does not exist. To begin with, the opposite could mean fostering a steadfast emotional posture that is opposed to anger, such as patience and compassion. In other words, the opposite of anger would not necessarily mean the absence of anger, but rather patience, for example. It is possible to understand this approach from the manner in which Vyāsa presents the concept of *avidyā* in Sūtra 2.5, not only as lack of wisdom or absence of knowledge, but also as a concrete positive perception in itself. Although the perception might be wrong, relative or partial, it is useful and functional in the relative dimension of existence in the world of phenomena.

Another example of the meaning of opposites is demonstrated by his use of the terms "friend" and "not-friend." The term "not-friend" does not necessarily indicate the absence of a friend. It points to a wide range of other possibilities: a person who was once a friend and is no longer one, or a person who was mistakenly perceived as a friend. It could also refer to the more concrete opposite of the term "friend": an enemy, or someone who is offensive, hostile or harmful. If so, Patañjali does not necessarily limit the concept of the opposite to its logical negative but leaves the concept of opposites open to reasonable possibilities. For example, patience, empathy and compassion may all be considered the opposite of anger. Thus, the method of *pratipakṣa bhāvanā* is not necessarily limited to a specific opposite of the moral principles of yoga that the practitioner violated or is about to violate.

Repetition of Affirmations as a Popular Concept of *Pratipakṣa Bhāvanā*

Pratipakṣa bhāvanā has been frequently misrepresented as a limited and reductive concept. Consider the example presented by the famous guitarist Carlos Santana. For Santana, one must simply eliminate negative impulses and replace them with positive ones, and avoid negative thoughts and focus instead on positive statements. This, he asserts, is how negative thoughts evaporate. What had seemed to be an impossible goal is actually attainable. He says, "Where is it that you often feel stuck? Take a moment to sit quietly and identify this clearly. Make the exact opposite your sincere incantation for the rest of the day. If it is sadness, then the repeated thought is *I am happy*. If it is tension, then the thought is *I am relaxed*. If it is anger, then *I am patient*, and so on."[8]

This lesson reflects popular New Age thinking which trivializes or flattens the method of *pratipakṣa bhāvanā* into the mere repetition of positive affirmations. It is as if the repetition of these positive statements had the effect of inserting them into the mind, convincing it of their truthfulness. The process promises to improve one's health and self-esteem and reduce anxiety, negative feedback and the use of psychological defense mechanisms.

Some researchers doubt the efficacy of the recitation of positive affirmations. They believe that repeating these statements may benefit some people, such as those with already high self-esteem, but it may actually have an adverse effect on those who need it most. They found that exaggerated compliments and unreasonable positive statements such as "I am strong and confident," or "I completely accept myself" can trigger conflicting thoughts in people with low self-esteem.[9]

That is, in order for positive *saṃskāras* to be internalized and assimilated, they must resonate with similar *saṃskāras* already imprinted in one's mind, even in low intensity. In other words, internalizing positive *saṃskāras* will succeed only when they come together with similar and already existing and resonating *saṃskāras*, not where such *saṃskāras* do not exist at all. Thus, in Santana's example, if the angry person does not already have a reservoir of positive *saṃskāras* of patience, then his attempt to internalize statements that cultivate patience will hardly work, if at all.

When positive statements are in conflict with one's self-perception, the mind will reject them and the original self-perception of low self-esteem will become even stronger. For example, people who perceive themselves as unpopular report that when they tell themselves something they do not really believe in (for example, that they are loved and popular), their negative self-perception does not improve, but rather becomes even more negative.

Apparently, positive statements fail to shift negative self-perception because they focus only on the conscious layer of the mind. If what we are trying to achieve by validating positive affirmation clashes with a deeply stored negative self-perception, then the attempt to transplant a positive affirmation will create an internal conflict. The internal conflict consumes many mental and physical resources, and the final result is a negative self-perception that only grows stronger.[10]

Controlling Destructive Instinctive Impulses as a Traditional Concept of *Pratipakṣa Bhāvanā*

In the opinion of the learned yogi Ramamurti Mishra,[11] *pratipakṣa bhāvanā* helps to control destructive instinctive impulses, as it provides a defensive response. By choosing a position contrary to the impulse, the mind tries to extinguish the impulse. The mind makes a substitution and consciously tries to wear it. Moreover, it helps achieve the ultimate goal of yoga, as it contributes to the purification of mental processes—to their transformation or cessation—on the way to discovering the true Self.

According to Mishra, dealing with destructive instinctive impulses increases the awareness of the pain and suffering they cause. He does not develop this interpretation into a practical method, not even in his chapter dedicated to psychological exercises, but merely outlines the method's principles. However, in my understanding, his interpretation is intended to suppress what is perceived as destructively negative thought or emotion. He argues that this capability varies greatly from person to person, depending on the intensity of their thoughts and the negative and destructive feelings. He does not question the effectiveness of the method; that is, he does not ask whether the willful removal or suppression of thoughts and unwanted feelings helps a person avoid a mental state he does not wish to experience.

Scholars in the field of psychology, such as Wegner and Wenzlaff, believed that the strategy of emotional suppression is ineffective and leads to the opposite effect; that is, to the continuation of the very mental state of mind that one is hoping to avoid.[12] Their conclusion is based on a meta-analysis of quantitative and qualitative studies in diverse fields of study, including the fields of emotions, memory, interpersonal processes, physio-psychological responses and psychopathology.[13] Wegner and Wenzlaff found that the desire to inhibit any thought or fear of such a thought leads to increased preoccupation with it, resulting in its intensification.[14] The heightened preoccupation with a thought evokes the moods associated with the event or the situations that created and perpetuated it. Moreover, suppressing a certain thought evokes the mood that preceded its suppression, causing the undesirable mood to return.

A finding of one of the studies showed that participants who experienced emotional stress and were instructed to relax became physically aroused or agitated. Other participants who experienced emotional stress but were not instructed to relax did not experience physical arousal. It was also found that high blood pressure was common in people with a chronic tendency to suppress their anger, a physio-psychological finding that also indicates that the suppression of emotions has negative physical consequences.[15] The suppression of emotions requires constant mental effort to compensate for the gap between the negative feeling itself and the feeling one desires. Persistent suppression affects the immune system and impairs its functioning, and this can have a negative effect on one's health.[16] In addition, the suppression of emotions may create internal stress, which in turn may affect immune system functions.[17]

It seems that even among those who are highly motivated to control their cravings—of drugs, alcohol, cigarettes or excessive eating, for example—the attempt to suppress their appetite results in the opposite effect. Attempting to suppress thoughts about physical pain, even about pain that is anticipated (such as before a medical procedure) leads to the opposite result, because suppressing thoughts cannot reduce or eliminate suffering. This conclusion is also true with regard to the memories we carry with us which usually persist even when we wish to forget.[18]

That is not to say that the suppression of certain emotions or tendencies is entirely ineffective or unnecessary. On the contrary, there are circumstances in which suppression is critical, such as the suppression of violence by a violent person. The question of whether suppression of thought and emotion is effective in reducing pain and suffering requires additional research. Nevertheless, for our purposes Wegner and Wenzlaff's findings present a significant challenge to Mishra's interpretation of *pratipakṣa bhāvanā*.

Reexamining the Traditional Conceptual Framework

Psychologist John Welwood describes the case of a patient who regularly experienced anger and frustration in her marriage.[19] In a state of despair, she turned to her guru for advice. He advised her not to be angry with her husband but to treat him with generosity and friendship. On the face of it, this advice is in line with Patañjali's teachings: "Through practice of friendliness [*maitrī*], compassion [*karuṇā*], joy [*muditā*], and equanimity [*upekṣa*] toward the happy, the suffering, the virtuous, and the unvirtuous (respectively), consciousness is clarified."[20]

She felt relieved by the guru's advice, for it suited her defensiveness against feelings of anger. Anger frightened her; she felt threatened by it and refused to deal with it. The instruction to express feelings of friendship and compassion was for her a spiritual bypass. But this only intensified her sense of helplessness and her frustration with married life.

The guru's advice was compatible with interpretations that consider *pratipakṣa bhāvanā* a method of adopting a contrary position to negative and destructive impulses in order to extinguish them and replace the negative tendency with another mental attitude. However, this method was not effective for Welwood's patient.

According to Welwood, the advice was given to her without taking into account her difficulty in suppressing and managing her intense anger. It turns out that she had been abused by her father in childhood.

Whenever she expressed anger about the way he treated her, he would slap her and send her to her room. He wanted to silence her expressions of anger and delegitimize them. Because of her fear of her father, she learned to suppress her anger, and instead tried to please others and be a "good girl."[21]

Her father's severe reaction left an intense impression on her, and as a result certain *saṃskāras* were etched in her mind, such as "when I'm angry, I'm in danger," "I'm unwanted when I'm angry," and "I'm not loved when I'm angry." These *saṃskāras* led to a *vāsanā*, a behavior pattern of avoiding anger and confrontation. This pattern made her submissive, always seeking to please others in order to gain their affection and feel a sense of belonging. The suppression of emotions and impulses associated with fear and aggression can therefore be an attempt to avoid confrontation, since confrontation may jeopardize affection and approval. Confrontation may also harm the attempt to create harmonious unity.[22] Thus, Welwood's patient would not express her anger toward her partner due to the hurtful fear associated with her *saṃskāras* of being unsafe and unloved.

The more she tried to apply the opposite practice, the more frustrated and helpless she became. The *saṃskāras* associated with her childhood experiences demonstrated that the advice she received did not suit her, because of her difficulty in coping with her undercurrents of anger. This difficulty raised questions about her ability to act assertively or to conduct an intimate dialogue with her partner and to still be loved, even in her anger.

Introspection as a Contemporary Concept of the *Pratipakṣa Bhāvanā*

The method of *pratipakṣa bhāvanā* is more than the repetition of positive statements or affirmations, as Carlos Santana would have us believe. Contrary to Mishra's interpretation, it is also more than a suppression of negative and destructive thoughts and feelings. Feuerstein argues that the practitioner may develop the method of *pratipakṣa bhāvanā* into a long, in-depth inquiry about the underlying motives of negative thoughts and emotions surfacing in his mind.[23] The exploration of thoughts and emotions depends on their importance for the practitioner, their frequency, intensity and the extent to which they are compulsive or difficult to change. For example, the occurrence of anger will only be examined if it is a consistent, stubborn and repetitive pattern intended to harm oneself and others, not a sporadic occurrence or an episodic expression of annoyance. According to Feuerstein, the method of cultivating the opposite implies a gradual ongoing application of certain guidelines. Its application enhances the cultivation of positive moral principles by integrating the recollection of the moral principles of yoga with meditative inquiry.[24]

The method is also an in-depth inquiry into the negative thoughts and emotions and their opposite; namely, the examination of the content and implications of the two opposites. Take for example a person who makes a friendly gesture to another person and gets no response. He might feel rejected, and rejection could cause insult or anger that might lead to confrontation. However, before confronting the other, the person should examine how truthful his gesture was. Perhaps the other person did not respond because they felt the gesture was inauthentic. This question deserves reflection, as does the consequence of a potential confrontation.

For Mehta, the essence of the method of *pratipakṣa bhāvanā* is to investigate the causes of affliction, and to examine the specific habitual tendencies of acceptance and rejection of the hidden motives underlying these causes.[25] In other words, a cause of affliction such as rejection can be expressed in the tendency to be angry, because when a person is angry it means that he does not accept a given situation, but prefers another, more desirable one. Mental imprints are like the undercurrents beneath these psychological processes, and when they come in contact with a certain stimulus, they awaken and dictate an action according to one's inclinations and patterns of behavior. If so, the *pratipakṣa bhāvanā* is about tracing the mental imprints that motivate people to act under their influence.

British Indologist Edwin Francis Bryant also claims that *pratipakṣa bhāvanā* is a kind of insight meditation which enables a yoga practitioner to modify and change his *saṃskāras* formation.[26] For him, *saṃskāras* that can silence and still the mind transcend the *saṃskāras* that carry pain. In *Satipatthana*, mindfulness meditation, the practitioner learns to identify thought processes and observe them, either during meditation or day-to-day activities, and label them as general concepts. For example, certain sounds or sights will be labeled "sensation." It is sufficient to name the sensation, its source, or the cause of its appearance, there is no need for further elaboration. This form of meditation is intended to bring about a breakthrough: the experience of a mind devoid of any content, including the sense of self. In relation to Bryant's interpretation, its primary intention is to bring about the awareness of sensations and feelings, and the ability to see them as they are, without judgment. Thus, it is possible to filter out what prevents the mind from coalescing into a peaceful state.

Observing the Consequences of Thoughts and Behaviors as the Classic Concept of *Pratipakṣa Bhāvanā*

While Feuerstein and Mehta consider the method an investigation into the nature of negative thoughts and feelings and an inquiry into the motives underlying them, Bryant views it as a kind of insight meditation. Vyāsa presents a broader and deeper psychological position, and in his commentary on Sūtra 2.34 he explains the method within the context of emotions. Here is the Sūtra: "To cultivate the opposite is [to reflect upon the fact] that thoughts which contradict the *yamas* such as violent thoughts and so on, whether executed, planned to be executed, or even approved, whether driven by greed, anger or delusion, whether mild, moderate or intense, result in endless suffering [*duḥkha*] and ignorance [*ajñāna*]."[27]

Vyāsa indicates that when a yoga practitioner feels negative emotions such as hatred, or is overwhelmed by desires that cause pain and acts under their influence, he must cultivate opposite thoughts.[28] That is, he is required to focus his attention on the consequences of such thoughts and actions and to seek spiritual refuge in the moral principles of yoga. Thus, instead of Vyāsa instructing the practitioner to cultivate virtues such as love and compassion—virtues that are opposite to the cause of affliction of hatred—he instructs him to initiate a meditative inquiry about the consequences of thoughts and actions that inflict hatred. He argues that the thought that violating the moral principles of yoga brings about endless pain and ignorance is in fact the opposite thinking. Vyāsa presents an example: "On account of causing pain one suffers by going to the infernal regions or by being born an animal or being an evil spirit."[29] In other words, merely thinking about the consequences of the negative thoughts and actions is the practice of cultivating the opposite, as it opens a gap between the negative thoughts and actions and their results, so that the practitioner will not automatically fall under their influence. That gap can become even deeper and wider, for in thinking of the inevitable consequences of his thoughts and wrongdoings, the practitioner can understand the suffering he had caused or will cause to others and to himself. This gap allows him to cultivate an opposite way of thinking and behaving so that he is not repeatedly engrossed in negative thoughts and actions.

This reversal—the practice or the cultivation of the opposite—is the focus of yoga practice, and it enables us to shift our inner gaze from negative thoughts and feelings caused by certain circumstance to the mind itself, and to adopt a reflective state of mind. For Vyāsa, the practice is not merely about reciting positive affirmations that are contrary to thoughts, actions and feelings that violate the moral principles of yoga. In the practice that he prescribes, there is no inquiry into the underlying motives for these thoughts, feelings and actions. For him, the practice is about focusing attention and reflecting on the outcome of negative actions and emotions, and on the understanding of their karmic implications: locking the practitioner into the vicious cycle of suffering.

Reflection on Consequences Generates Feelings that Support Cultivation of the Opposite

Vyāsa's commentary to Sūtra 2.34 implies a therapeutic process. Reflecting on thoughts, behavior, or emotions that are contrary to yogic ethics and are about theft, lust and greed can evoke memories of hurt to oneself and others. Such memories may evoke feelings, such as self-honesty, sensitivity to the pain of others and remorse. These feelings have the power to widen the gap between negative thoughts and actions and their consequences, untying their connecting lines of causation and deepening the gap into an abyss.

For yoga practitioners, self-honesty means turning their gaze toward their prevailing emotions, observing them as they are by lessening the ego's alertness and tendency to protect or defend attributes and images with which they identify, and by accepting their own vulnerability. These emotions cause pain, and usually the tendency to defend oneself from pain leads to blaming others for one's thoughts or actions. Nevertheless, one should not evade or deny these emotions.

Self-honesty implies understanding the meaning of each hurt. It is the ability to sense the distress each hurt raises by naming it. Thus, the practitioner starts by defusing the wounds of their emotional charge so that they do not accumulate or become a seedbed for emotions such as anger, vengeance, fear or shame. Being honest allows us to admit to ourselves that we are having feelings we do not want to have, feelings that conflict with our desires, our belief system, and our self-perception. A mind rooted in self-honesty does not recoil from having and bearing such emotions, and it does not seek to evade them. Such a mind is committed to the world of emotions. It assumes responsibility for their consequences and does not blame others.

Sometimes the immediate attempt to observe or analyze emotions that we do not want to feel, or to talk about or focus upon, is actually an attempt to avoid them and an expression of our unwillingness to accord them a place in our emotional life. Self-honesty allows these internal defense mechanisms to be suspended and their alertness to subside. Then intimacy is exposed. One acknowledges one's negative emotions and actions, accepts responsibility for their consequences, and thus becomes exposed to one's deepest sense of humanity, becoming closer to oneself. This is the definition of true self-honesty, rather than to what is merely a personal or social manipulation. True self-honesty is not intended to increase social capital or elevate one's self-image, as in the case of the person who seeks to please others or create a sense of belonging in order to promote personal interests or business status.

In American Benedictine monk and scholar Columba Stewart's research of the literature of the desert fathers, the fourth-century Christian monks who lived in the deserts of Egypt, he describes powerful accounts of radical self-honesty. He makes it clear that such honesty "lifts the screen" and exposes our inner demons and the secrets we keep.[30] If our secrets and demons have no place to hide, they cannot continue to raise obsessive desires. By virtue of radical honesty, compulsive desires are brought to light in the arena of truth, where their painful nature becomes clear just a moment before they become established in the mind, distorting it and obscuring its clarity. Obviously, these demons are not real creatures. They represent daily emotions and problems, from fear, to illness, depression, anxiety, trauma, difficulties in relationships and addiction. Self-honesty begins with recognizing these demons and understanding that they inhabit one's mind and make demands upon it.

In the context of the *Yoga Sūtras*, self-honesty refers to the honesty of a person with himself; however, the Christian monks realized honesty within their relationships. They openly confessed their pain and frustration to their older and more experienced colleagues, exposing their vulnerability in order to dissolve the last layers of shame that clung to them.

Meditation deals with harmful thoughts that stem from greed, anger or delusion. It is not enough to practice true self-honesty in order to create the gap that can disconnect these harmful thoughts from their concrete expression or manifestation. Yet, under certain circumstances such harmful thoughts have the potential to become amplified and repeated countless times, causing people to act out of greed, anger or delusion.

Another aspect emerges from the process implied by Vyāsa's commentary of practicing the opposite as reflecting on the consequences of harmful thoughts and actions. It seems that this is a meditation that focuses on being sensitive to the suffering caused to others by the practitioner's greed, anger or delusion. This sensitivity also affects the practitioner himself, for as Patañjali implicitly points out in Sūtra 2.34, resonating others' pain and suffering has the potential to change our attitudes and behavior, and to dilute thoughts of greed, anger or confusion.

Sensitivity to the suffering or pain of others means being able to put ourselves in their shoes. This is the foundation of empathy; however,

I deliberately chose not to use this term. Empathy is the ultimate basis for healthy interactions within personal relationships, but in social contexts we generally have empathy with those to whom we are attracted, or with those who seem similar to us, rather than with those from different geographical or cultural backgrounds. For example, we may watch a movie that will evoke empathy toward a character on the screen who is suffering, bringing us to tears, but as soon as we leave the cinema empathy evaporates and we return to our old ways. We do not notice the beggar on the street corner, we respond with frustration to the friend who watched the film with us who is not aware of our mood caused by the film and insists on having a conversation with us. The selectivity of empathy is incompatible with the cultivation of the yogic opposite.[31]

However, in our context, sensitivity to others involves the ability to observe reality through their eyes, to feel their painful experiences and to participate in their pain without identifying with them. After all, the participation in others' pain or distress, even if such feelings may be weak, are not fundamentally different from the pain of others.[32] Sensitivity expressed through understanding the pain of others is not a cognitive understanding devoid of emotion. The sensitivity that arises in the face of the pain of others plays a significant role in the practice of the opposite.

This sensitivity is more than an instinctive response, for it can be cultivated, directed and refined through the imagination. Writing about empathy, psychologist Paul Bloom quotes President Barack Obama:

> To see the world through the eyes of those who are different from us—the child who is hungry, the steelworker who's been laid off, the family who lost the entire life they built together when the storm came to town. When you think like this, when you choose to broaden your ambit of concern and empathize with the plight of others, whether they are close friends or distant strangers, it becomes harder not to act, harder not to help.[33]

Obama's words indicate that such sensitivity is an active gesture, and it concerns not only our relatives but also foreigners.

Obama emphasizes the social aspect of sensitivity and its positive power in establishing goodness in the world. In the context of the yoga practitioner's cultivation of the opposite, it means seeing the pain of others, understanding that he has caused it, and acknowledging his responsibility for it. Sensitivity to the suffering of others and the participation in their pain is directed not only toward the immediate environment of the practitioner, his family or his community, but also toward strangers. One example is understanding the implications of purchasing products produced under exploitative and inhumane employment conditions in a distant continent and understanding their effect on the prolonged misery of workers.

Cultivating the opposite, thinking about the consequences of the act, and the injustice that the yoga practitioner has caused himself or others, may generate another important emotion: remorse. Remorse is the deep and painful feeling for actions that shouldn't have been done. Remorse may arise not only following an action, but also in response to *not* acting; for example, not saving a person from drowning. According to Australian clinical psychologist Michael Proeve and Australian law scholar Steven Tudor,[34] the feeling of remorse belongs to a family of emotions that includes sorrow, guilt and shame. These emotions usually cause people to become withdrawn and to regret or avoid circumstances that may trigger these emotions. They will refrain from committing an act that constitutes an injustice to others or harm to themselves. In the context of yoga, if they committed a harmful act they would be engulfed with disturbing feelings, because they did not meet the standards set for themselves, and they would fear that their weakness would adversely affect their karma. According to Vyāsa, such a karma may cause one to suffer "by going to infernal regions or being born as an animal or as an evil spirit," and a "fatal disease on account of which he goes on suffering continuously."[35]

It is necessary to distinguish between remorse and other feelings, such as sorrow, guilt, shame and embarrassment. Shame is different from the other emotions, for it is a painful one that arises from the sense of failure in achieving an ideal state. It envelops the whole person and mainly revolves around a pattern of behavior that he wishes to adopt, and withdrawal from situations that will arouse his shame. It is often thought that embarrassment is a lesser form of shame, and like shame, it is less focused on oneself and more associated with social situations, such as coughing during a concert. Guilt stems from the assessment that a certain behavior is negative. It surfaces from the realization that one has caused mental or physical distress or violated one's own moral code. Guilt can also arise from desire rather than action; for example, from the desire of another woman while in a relationship. Just wanting to be with someone else may harm one's current relationship, and it can cause as much guilt as the act itself. Sometimes a person feels guilty for not helping others enough or because he is better off than others; for example, by surviving a disaster while losing one's loved ones. In any case, guilt relates to the individual's sense of responsibility and to his intent to correct what has been distorted, sometimes through material or emotional compensation.

Remorse is not that different from sorrow. The emphasis here is on the deep, disturbing and unrelenting grief that a person feels for committing a harmful act, directly or indirectly, affecting people he identifies with and knows, or a particular population, or animals. We cannot dwell on that sorrow, but we must internalize its moral message with seriousness and clarity.

A central characteristic of remorse related to cultivating the opposite is its ability to change one's self-perception. A person who is aware of the consequences of his actions and accepts responsibility for them will decide not to repeat the painful action. He will choose to act differently and to internalize mental and behavioral changes. Remorse is associated with sensitivity to the pain of others and to their feelings. A person feels regret after causing injustice, and in the awakening of his conscience there is a great deal of emotional power that can generate a change in his patterns of thinking and behaving.

In other words, in the practice of the opposite, thinking about the consequences of the actions stems from the remorse and its innate pain that can be intense and sometimes even overwhelming. Pain plays an important role in practice and is inseparable from thinking about the consequences of actions. The sensation of pain is characterized by its sharpness and vibrancy; it can feel like a bite or sting, or an internal storm, and it causes tension. These feelings do not stem from the emergence of an internal conflict, but rather from the personal involvement in the injustice done to others and from the desire to reject and avoid such involvement.[36] Such a pain, which is innate to the feeling of remorse, has a significant contribution to the awakening of emotional power that can cause a change in thinking and behavior.

Usually remorse is accompanied by a desire to ask forgiveness from others. However, the request for forgiveness of the injured is not mentioned at all in Vyāsa's commentary to Sūtra 2.34, on which this discussion is based, or even in other interpretations of this Sūtra. It appears, then, that in Vyāsa's and Patañjali's views, demonstration of remorse in yoga may be internal and expressed within oneself. However, yoga practitioners can of course choose to expand their expressions of remorse and add confession, apology and forgiveness in the context of social interactions. Such expressions of remorse can help to establish and sustain a mental-behavioral change that practitioners may wish to cultivate to alleviate the pain of others and ease their mental burden.

Reflecting back on Welwood's patient, now in connection with Feuerstein's and Mehta's interpretations of *pratipakṣa bhāvanā*, we see that the patient's problem was not the anger itself, but the fear of its expression and of its consequences. As opposed to the guru's advice to cultivate feelings of friendship and compassion toward her partner, practicing the opposite may mean cultivating the courage to express anger out of maturity and sensitivity to the needs and feelings of her partner, with the understanding that it is her fundamental right to feel and express emotions, even if they are perceived as negative ones. Expressing and sharing these emotions are learned skills that must be cultivated, since they are essential for maintaining a healthy and intimate relationship. Sharing will prevent negative emotions from turning into latent hostility that can gradually destroy the trust and connection between a couple.

Bryant sees *pratipakṣa bhāvanā* as a type of insight meditation, but this perspective is consistent with the patient's defense mechanism of avoidance out of fear of her anger and its consequences. Had she applied the *pratipakṣa bhāvanā* according to Bryant's interpretation, she would have identified and observed her anger, thus holding it off or withdrawing from it. In this way, insight-meditation practice can become a spiritual bypass when one refuses to confront or deal with the anger, but anger is a cause of affliction, a mental activity that captivates people in *avidyā*.

Insight meditation, according to Bryant's interpretation, primarily aims to identify feelings and observe them without involvement. Even though this reflective component is a dominant constituent of *pratipakṣa bhāvanā*, it did not seem adequate for the patient at this stage of her life. Instead, it seemed more appropriate for her to learn to pay attention to her anger so that she could move beyond the usual pattern of self-oppression. This would allow her to reveal her inner strength and treat her husband more assertively than before.

And now the long-haired yogi approaches my window, glances at my computer screen, and nods at the reading of the sentence: "anger is a cause of affliction, a mental activity that captivates people in *avidyā*." He reminds me that anger has nothing to do with the real Self, so I must now stop trying to dedicate these lines to anger, which in themselves are but mental processes, additional discursive waves that preoccupy the mind. Apparently, he speaks out of his presence, abiding in the real Self, while I am here in the relative reality, where anger, as a cause of affliction, will recur and cause suffering to others and to a person who fears it, or expresses it as a blind and hurtful wave of rage. The long-haired yogi insists. He says that the separation of the two realities, relative and absolute, has nothing to do with the real Self. It is just another thought that distorts the perception of reality. I must abandon it too, and bring it to cessation. I recommune and gather inside myself, becoming still and silent for a long while. Yet I do not let go completely, and from the edges of my silence I see, for moments, faces of distant and close relatives and foreigners who express pain because of my actions and the actions of others. Mental pictures of pain bring me back to the Sūtras.

In my view, Vyāsa's commentary demonstrates that reflecting on the consequences of anger can lead to self-honesty, sensitivity and closeness to the other who is in distress. Anger, with all of its shades of intensities and the remorse felt as a result of the behavior and actions it causes, could enable Welwood's patient to undergo a process that would help her cultivate an opposite by practicing the courage to express anger. She would recognize her fear of expressing anger, and understand the meaning of repressing her anger toward her partner and the significance of its raw expression as a wave of emotion. She might also take into consideration her partner's feelings of pain and insult. Her remorse will gnaw at her, awakening her conscience. This great emotional force may change the content of her thoughts and behavior. It could stop her from being driven automatically by fear of anger and open a window for new expressions of assertiveness. In practicing the opposite, there is a significant decrease of fuel supplied to the causes of affliction. If so, *pratipakṣa bhāvanā* may be a combination of thinking and reflecting about the results of thoughts and actions that violate the principles of yogic morality, in a manner that generates self-honesty, sensitivity to others, and remorse, while tracing one's underlying motives. Such practice allows for such a dual process.

In the context of Welwood's patient, the process may on the one hand reduce the supply of fuel to her anger, prevent accumulation and solidification of negative karma, and help her develop compassion for her partner. On the other hand, the practice of the opposite, which in this case is the search for the underlying motives of her anger, may allow her to cultivate the courage to express anger and thereby help to dissolve it toward deepening her intimacy with her partner. Cultivating the courage to express anger may free her from the burdens of fear and help her to acquire self-understanding, compassion and assertiveness.

Furthermore, cultivating the opposite functions also as an indirect coping mechanism with the causes of affliction, since attention is diverted from them and focused onto their consequences. By diverting attention from the causes of affliction, their fuel is depleted and the practitioner ceases to react to them. This widens the gap between negative thoughts and actions and their ability to influence the yoga practitioner. The yogi is less likely to be caught in emotional turmoil as the mental imprints are thinned, and he is less and less exposed to stimuli that may activate them. In that space, a window of openness is created that enables the emergence of new expressions of assertiveness.

This proposed process, *pratipakṣa bhāvanā*, corresponds with the two foundations of yoga practice prescribed by Patañjali: "The cessation of these *vṛttis* or instances of mental activity is accomplished through repetitive practice [*abhyāsa*] and dispassion [*vairāgya*]."[37] In the context of *pratipakṣa bhāvanā*, repeated activity (*abhyāsa*) is largely meditative, and is motivated by the desire to establish a stable and imperturbably still mind emptied of all mental activity in order to address directly the causes of affliction and cultivate their opposite. Repeated practice will gradually lead to stillness of mind and its emptying of any mental or emotional activity.

The practice is therefore directed at the causes of affliction, and the practitioner is determined to overcome them. Dispassion (*vairāgya*) is the absence of any tendency toward the causes of affliction, such as attraction and aversion, lack of interest, or indifference to them, in the context of their objects. In Vyāsa's view, dispassion progresses gradually, and consists of an uninvolved awareness with the causes of affliction, followed by contemplation on the opposite results.[38]

These two foundations—repeated activity as repetitive meditative effort and open uninvolved awareness—seem to contradict each other, but in fact they are complementary, for they are two forces that act simultaneously. An expression of simultaneity can be found not only in yoga but also in a host of other activities. For example, when playing the classical guitar, the fingers of the left hand find their way to the correct position on the fretboard in coordination with the fingers of the right hand, which are plucking the correct strings. As a result of persistent practice and steadfast concentration, both hands gradually produce the right sound with increasing ease. After a while it seems that the act of playing is almost effortless. The mind is hardly focused on the movement of the fingers. At this stage, making music becomes a creative and inspiring activity, not just the mechanical sounding of notes.

Repeated activity (*abhyāsa*) and open uninvolved awareness (*vairāgya*) are complementary forces in the physical dimension of yoga as well: āsana (yogic posture) is comfortably stable.[39] This means that the repeated active effort, as in *abhyāsa*, leads to maintaining a stable posture for long durations, and the practitioner is comfortable and relaxed in *vairāgya*. There is no striving for achievement related to performing the posture or judgment about its quality. All that is required of the practitioner is to remain in the mental gesture of *pratipakṣa bhāvanā*, cultivating the opposite; that is, repeatedly thinking about the consequences resulting from violations in thought or action of the yogic codes of conduct, generating self-honesty, empathy and remorse, but without attachment or a sense of identification with the circumstances.

If Welwood's patient exercises only the expression of anger, the anger may hurt others. Moreover, excessive attention to the exercise of cultivating courage in order to overcome the fear of expressing anger would fuel the *kleśa* instead of weakening it, implying a latent attachment to it. Without the second, reflective element of *vairāgya*, cultivating the opposite, which mainly includes an uninvolved contemplation of the results of the fear of anger or the actual results of the expression of anger, the probability of overcoming *kleśas* is limited. This goal then becomes difficult to achieve, since reflection helps dismantle and empty the *kleśas* of their potentiality. In other words, when one of these two foundations of practice (*abhyāsa* and *vairāgya*) is missing, the ability to overcome or dismantle a *kleśa* is impaired. Moreover, cultivation of the opposite based on the second foundation alone—dispassion or uninvolved awareness—is not sufficient. Contemplative uninvolved awareness alone will not enable the acquisition of new skills necessary to erode the *kleśas* and the suffering they cause. In other words, the patient may realize the consequences of not expressing her anger, or she might want to liberate herself from the fear of expressing anger, but she will need to learn a new skill and practice it repeatedly. She must cultivate the courage to express anger, assertively and in various ways, without harming others or their natural rights.

3

Pratipakṣa Bhāvanā as Imagining the Opposite

Sir Monier Monier-Williams (1819–1899) was the second Boden Professor of Sanskrit at Oxford University. In his Sanskrit–English dictionary,[1] there is another meaning to the Sanskrit word *bhāvanā*: to imagine. Redefining *bhāvanā* as imagining may shed new light on Patañjali's method of cultivating the opposite, *pratipakṣa bhāvanā*. We can learn about the connection between *bhāvanā*, meditation, and imagining from Indologist and Sanskritist David Shulman's work.[2] Shulman provided a comprehensive study of many aspects of the concept of *bhāvanā*: philosophical, grammatical, poetic and logical. In his book, he coined the term "yoga of imagination," referring to *bhāvanā* being synonymous with imagination.[3] He asserts that in the middle of the first millennium, the concept of the *bhāvanā* referred primarily to a focused meditation that was accompanied by visualization, in an attempt to give the deity, the visualized object of meditation, a vivid and real sense of presence.

Shulman illustrates the meaning of *bhāvanā* as imagining in a series of Tamil poems. One of the poems, written by a devotee of Shiva in the seventh century, is directed at the deity. The deity is created by means of a poem or mantra recitation and imagination; that is, the form and entire iconography of the deity that is the object of meditation is vividly constructed in the imagination. A poem from the eighth century suggests that the reader identify with Shiva as "honey flowing through the minds of those who imagine him." If so, it is possible to see *bhāvanā* as a situation that creates or constructs an inner mental picture of the deity as the object of meditation that inhabits the imagining mind. Because the concept of deity is usually mysterious and inaccessible, one attempts to give it presence through the act of imagining. At the same time, the act of meditative imagining seeks to nullify the objectification of the deity and strip the imagining devotee of his sense of subjectivity in order to allow the wisdom of deity to flow as honey in the mind that imagines him.[4]

A twelfth-century poem is dedicated to the tantric ritual of the deity Saundarya-lahari. In the poem, the purpose of the *bhāvanā* is to imagine the deity as one's real Self. The poem mentions visualization exercises and mantra recitations aimed at establishing focused attention to evoke the deity as an active presence. These exercises and mantra recitations represent one of the types of yoga of the imagination. They result in the awakening of the *kuṇḍalinī*, a force that enables the yogi to enter an ecstatic state of awakening and become acquainted with his true Self.[5]

Imagination is power, and its use within the tantric context lends a sense of presence to the object of meditation, either a god or a goddess. The real and vivid sense of presence reduces the subjective involvement in the process, suspends it, and allows for a merging with the deity as one's true Self. The merger as the integration or unification of meditating subject and meditated object enables the dawn of Self-knowledge.

British-Hungarian Indologist Csaba Kiss also translates *bhāvanā* as imagining; a meaning, he claims, that has a central significance in his philological study of *Matsyendrasahitā*, a thirteenth-century Sanskrit text of the Shaivite sect of yogis from southern India.[6] For him, *bhāvanā* as imagining is a meditative process focused on visualizing a deity, a process aimed at creating an identity or union between the meditating person and the object of meditation. Imagining involves intense emotion, which Kiss refers to as "empathy."[7] He concedes that the use of the term empathy is not entirely precise, but he uses it mainly to emphasize that the meditative process is not a mechanical one. That is to say, *bhāvanā* is not only an intense, vivid construction of the object of meditation as an imagined mental picture, but it is also accompanied by a strong emotional gesture. I would argue that this gesture is an expression of the intense yearning to merge with the object of meditation—god or goddess—and become freed from pain and suffering.

Shulman's and Kiss's examinations of *bhāvanā* in relation to the imagination refers to the period from the sixth to thirteenth centuries in southern India, and it revolves around meditative tantric methods. As Patañjali probably lived in the third or fourth century CE, his work has much in common with the *Sāṅkhya* school of Indian philosophy. Its system of thought is the framework for the *Yoga Sūtras*, including most of its varied interpretations or commentaries.[8]

The Sāṅkhya system of thought is based on a rational exploration of the elements in the world of phenomena (*prakṛti*), including the five elements, the senses, the mind and the ego. This inquiry culminates in focusing on the intellect, the source of inquiry. Once the essence of these elements becomes known, the Sāṅkhya philosopher realizes that the true Self is not part of the world of phenomena. Yoga is based on meditation and concentration that develops into direct perception, an intuitive, non-conceptual perception that transcends labels and discursive thought and leads to discerning wisdom between the world of phenomena and the real Self. This discernment culminates in disentanglement of the true Self from the web with which it is associated—the world of phenomena. In other words, *bhāvanā* is a meditation and a synonym for *dhyāna*, according to both yogic and tantric texts, but unlike Patañjali's yoga, the latter also contain specific rituals dedicated to specific deities, including components of imagination and emotion. At the same time, it would be reasonable to assume that the yogic practice of *Īśvara praṇidhāna* prescribed by Patañjali, which is devotion to the Lord, might also include components of imagination and emotion. However, such an assumption would need to be validated by rigorous research that is beyond the scope of this book.

The historical differences mentioned so far in the interpretations of *bhāvanā* and the reasonable notion about *Īśvara praṇidhāna* enrich and add various meanings to the concept, and it would be worthwhile examining how one should understand and apply practicing the opposite together with imagining the opposite. Such an examination allows us to explore the practice of the opposite in depth, and to understand how effective it is in addressing the *kleśas*, reducing the suffering and pain that they may cause.

Combining *bhāvanā* with imagining within the method of cultivating the opposite has a great deal of weight in practice, since imagining, which is intensive and vivid, has the potential to bring about desired results. It has the advantage of recalling vivid mental pictures of events, figures and places, even strangers and those unknown in one's imagination. In tantra yoga, the combination is expressed by making the deity into a real living presence in conjunction with attentive, pragmatic and methodical meditation.[9]

According to the dual practice, in imagining the opposite the practitioner creates a mental picture of an interaction or an event that usually causes him to respond with a charged reaction, either out of aversion or out of attraction. The practitioner is required to imagine himself acting differently in a similar situation, adopting a behavior that is the opposite of his habitual one. In his imagination, he observes the results of his behavior, honestly responds to what is happening, and relates sensitively to others who are also present in the imagined scene. In the face of pain or anger that he caused to arise in others, the practitioner feels remorse and decides wholeheartedly to change his ways. It is possible that during the process of reflecting on the pain caused to others, he may have thoughts that may lead to a defensive attitude, like "but he brought it on himself; it's his fault." This will divert the practitioner from the process. If so, deep internal honesty is very important to the success of the process, as it prevents further *kleśas* during exercise and helps to focus on the practice of the opposite.

In this process, it is also possible to try to simulate an opposite behavior to the one that caused others pain and suffering. Practicing the opposite combined with imagining is a powerful exercise in the sense that the practitioner is not only thinking about the event and the consequences of his behavior that violated the principles of yoga ethics, but also experiencing the atmosphere, smells, dialogues and body language of those present in the imagined scene. All of these contribute to an unmediated understanding of the event and its consequences while adopting the opposite. It is possible to conjure or retrieve not only mental images from the past, but also images of a possible future in which the moral principles of yoga are violated, whether intentionally or not.

Thus, a person who acknowledges and knows his motives, tendencies, behavior patterns and the stimuli that may trigger thoughts of harming others, may imagine a possible future event, feel it, and practice the opposite of the relevant *kleśa*, which repeatedly fails him. This process follows the principles of dual practice (tracing the motives and thinking of and imagining the results). Through this practice, he dilutes the karma associated with a certain cause of affliction, and also the karma that might be caused in the future. Through practice, he also thickens the *saṃskāras* of silence, or stillness. For example, a person who is aware of his tendency to be greedy or stingy, and knows its consequences for himself and others, may decide to practice generosity. He may imagine a future situation in which he walks the streets of the city and sees a beggar who approaches him asking him for money. He would see himself reach into his pocket, pull out a coin or a note, or even buy a meal for the beggar. In this process, thoughts may arise that seek to preserve the old pattern of behavior of greed and miserliness, such as "why should I make donations? I pay taxes so that the government will take care of those beggars." But here self-honesty is very important, and it can bring the practitioner back to the process of imagining the opposite and dealing with his habitual tendency (*vāsanā*). Such practice reverberates through Sūtra 2.16: "Suffering which has not yet come can be prevented."[10] In other words, meditation that incorporates imagining a future event that involves suffering has the power to prevent or dilute the karma that may arise from such an afflictive event.

Thus, the *pratipakṣa bhāvanā* as imagining the opposite is relevant for all times: past, present and future. It enables the practitioner to dismantle emotional burdens arising from negative thoughts and actions and undo them. Such a practice is consistent with the time ranges described in the Sūtra:

> To cultivate the opposite is [to reflect upon the fact] that thoughts which contradict the *yamas*, such as violent thoughts and so on, whether executed, planned to be executed, or even approved, whether driven by greed, anger, or delusion, whether mild, moderate, or intense, result in endless suffering [*duḥkha*] and ignorance [*ajñāna*].[11]

Welwood's case study of the patient who experienced anger and frustration in her marriage illustrated how the method of *pratipakṣa bhāvanā* was intended to cultivate the opposite of anger, a cause of affliction in the category of aversion or rejection, *dveṣa*. Now I will focus on *pratipakṣa bhāvanā* as imagining the opposite of greed, a cause of affliction in the category of attraction or attachment, *rāga*. Greed is an emotion related to jealousy and envy. American Psychotherapist Joseph Berke described it succinctly as a primal emotional impulse which is most harmful, a man's merciless desire to take for himself what others have, to possess and hoard objects of desire.[12]

A greedy man thinks that what he craves is good and valuable. An envious person does not wish to hoard objects of desire, but rather to prevent others from having them. According to the Austrian-British psychoanalyst Melanie Klein (1882–1960), greed is an insatiable hunger or craving that can never be fulfilled, for the objects of desire are beyond what one really needs. It is a destructive force directed at one's inner being and born of a fundamental and inexhaustible sense of deprivation. When the feeling of want is deep and powerful, it can fixate one to obsessively seek objects of desire in order to compensate for the feeling of deprivation. Life then becomes a journey of amassing objects of desire.[13]

The practice of *pratipakṣa bhāvanā* can be thought of as imagining the opposite of greed. I will return to Dickens's novella *A Christmas Carol* to illustrate this concept. Although the story is interwoven with elements of fantasy and imagination, it also describes the characters, events, activities and day-to-day experiences that can be explored through the lens of the psychology of yoga. Dickens realistically described scenes of modern life; at the same time, his use of fantasy allowed him to compress time and apply moral dimension to the full cycle of life.

At the beginning of the story, we learn that Scrooge is greedy and miserly, a man without imagination. As a child he read *Arabian Nights* and *Robinson Crusoe*, but as an adult he no longer imagines, he is only greedy. In the opinion of American researcher of British literature, narrative theory, and the psychology of reading Mary-Catherine Harrison, Dickens's story deals with the psychological and social transformation of Scrooge, and it revolves around imagination, a feature that encourages sensitivity to others because it allows one to put oneself in the shoes of others and feel connected.[14] Adopting another person's perspective through imagination creates emotions such as remorse and compassion, skills that Scrooge acquires when he finds himself haunted by ghosts.

On Christmas Eve, Scrooge is visited by three spirits who each lead him to different scenes of his life, bringing about his transformation. Although the ghosts in the story are imaginary, they represent a certain aspect of the I-am-ness or the ego, the part that is self-aware and ethical and understands the consequences of one's actions. This faculty of one's ego emerges in moments when one's mind becomes flexible and open to change, for it understands that the usual ways in which it regulates itself and the forces that operate within and without it are no longer effective. In Scrooge's case, when he meets Marley's ghost his overwhelming experience of anxiety and shock shatters his coping mechanisms, allowing his mind to become flexible and open.[15] He recognizes that he cannot escape reality. This concrete sense of inescapability is the source of the power to effect change. At the sight of his nephew, feelings of sorrow engulfed him, and he tried to suppress his longing for connection by doing the opposite: showing hostility toward Fred.

An analogy to these moments, when one's mind becomes flexible and receptive to change, can be found in Sūtra 1.1: "Now the instruction about yoga." "Now" represents a moment of self-awareness that arises in a person. He realizes that he can no longer think and act as he did in the past, because his thinking patterns and manner of behavior caused suffering and pain for himself and others. It is a moment of self-awareness that arises in the *sattvic* spacious and pure quality of the *buddhi*, one's seat of intelligence. It is a window in time when one can turn his gaze toward yoga, redirecting it inward, away from the tendency of objectification. It is a moment in which it is possible to overcome the tendency to fixate on the objects of desire that provoke the causes of affliction, a moment in which one can extricate oneself from the vicious cycle of *samsara*.

Classical and contemporary commentators of the *Yoga Sūtras* believe that the word "now" in Sūtra 1.1, found in the opening of texts, is a welcome word that expresses blessings. It is an analog to the *Om*, the first syllable or the primal sound from which all has begun.[16] Others believe that once the student has acquired the basic skills and moral foundations, "now" becomes the appropriate time to learn the teachings of yoga. Some scholars argue that the word "now" marks a transition from previously discussed texts to the text of yoga, and Vijñānabhikṣu believes that it also marks a difference or hierarchy between these texts.[17]

I believe that "now" is not just a moment of self-awareness, or a window in time when one can turn one's gaze toward yoga and walk in its path. It is also a defining, formative moment, continuously renewed, in which a conscious change takes place when one practices the opposite. This moment is the basis for the practice of yoga, the moment when both fundamental components of yoga are practiced simultaneously—repetitive meditation (*abhyāsa*) and uninvolved awareness (*vairāgya*)—as two forces that operate at the same time. This refers to the joining of repetitive, mostly meditative activity, which gradually leads to silencing the mind, emptying it of all its mental or emotional activity with uninvolved contemplation.

Grinshpon points to a connection between personal and interpersonal crises and the emergence of the desire for self-liberating knowledge that is described in the *Upaniṣads*. The emergence of the desire for liberation takes place in such defining moments, moments in which a transformation takes place. To illustrate this point, he presents a story from the *Bṛhadāraṇyaka Upaniṣad*, a story that takes place in the Vedic society of the eighth century BCE. In this story, the sage Yājñavalkya informs Maitreyī, his childless wife, that he is leaving for the forest in the pursuit Self-realization. Before he leaves, Maitreyī asks him to teach her about the real Self. An intimate dialogue develops between them about the true Self. Many commentators and scholars see it as a story of spirituality and deep intimacy. But beneath the surface, the story is saturated with conflict. Maitreyī is angry and confused. She feels abandoned and suffers the pain of being childless, and therefore will receive no inheritance according to the customs of the time. The inheritance will be passed on to Yājñavalkya's other wife, the mother of their children, and Maitreyī is considered a miserable widow who is physically alive but socially almost dead. In that moment of crisis, Maitreyī turns to her husband Yājñavalkya with a bitter, silent anger and asks him to guide her toward the immortal knowledge of the Self.[18] This crucial moment is the moment of "now" mentioned in Sūtra 1.1, that instant in which the path unfolds toward Self-knowledge, and in our context this refers to the path of yoga.

I return to Scrooge's story. In the first moment of "now," the first spirit, the Ghost of Christmas Past, takes him back to scenes of his childhood and youth. These scenes evoke tender feelings from the greedy old man, and he recalls his innocent childhood. Waves of painful emotions come over him as he recalls his long-term physical and emotional neglect. He is overcome with memories that fill him with feelings of affection and love, feelings that had shut down after the death of his sister. His heart aches when he sees his joyful ex-fiancée with her family.

The second spirit, the Ghost of Christmas Present, takes Scrooge to the poor family of his clerk, Bob Cratchit. He witnesses their preparations for their Christmas celebration and sees Bob's youngest son, Tiny Tim, ill and lacking medical care. He is engulfed with feelings of concern when he understands that his miserly unwillingness to pay Bob a decent wage has contributed to Tiny Tim's difficult health condition. Seeing the images that surface in his mind, Scrooge experiences emotional and physical pain and his resistance subsides, and with it his deep fear of deprivation. He becomes less and less defensive. The scenes he envisions of the Cratchit family elicit painful remorse. In these mental images, the physical and emotional neglect that Scrooge suffered and the motives for his greed become evident. Through the lens of the psychology of yoga, it seems that Scrooge undergoes a process similar to cultivating the opposite—he reflects and understands the consequence of his past and present neglect: causing suffering to himself and others. This understanding generates self-honesty, sensitivity and closeness to others in distress, and remorse for his past negative thoughts and actions. All this seems similar to the teaching in Sūtra 2.34, which relates to reflecting and thinking about the consequences of painful thoughts, behaviors and events that have taken place in the past.

The third spirit, the Ghost of Christmas Yet to Come, presents Scrooge with the difficult scenes that could take place if he does not learn his lessons. In one of those scenes he sees the death of Tiny Tim, and in another his own derelict grave. These sights prompt him to change his ways in the hope of stopping "the shadows of what can happen." In these mental images he can see the possible ramifications of his greed, for himself and others. From the perspective of yoga psychology, it seems that Scrooge underwent a process similar to cultivating the opposite, which is about reflecting and thinking on the consequences of painful thoughts, behaviors and events, and generating empathy toward oneself and others in distress.

Scrooge wakes up on Christmas morning, spends the day with his nephew's family, and anonymously sends the Cratchit family a gift of a large turkey. He has become a different person overnight: kind, generous and compassionate. At the end of the story, Dickens confirms that Scrooge's transformation is deep and permanent.

The story clearly illustrates how effective *pratiaksha bhāvanā* can be and how it might be implemented by integrating imagination into the method. Imagining enables one to raise thoughts and feel moods and emotions. It allowed Scrooge to reexperience painful actions associated with the three periods in his life, and to see their consequences. As a result, one can develop sensitivity and closeness to others and feel real remorse or forgiveness. This process ultimately alleviates the emotional burden linked to the causes of affliction.

Imagining the Opposite, an Exercise

The consideration of the practice of cultivating the opposite through imagining in light of Dickens's work could imply the following exercise. It is capable of weakening and thinning habitual tendencies or the causes of affliction.

1. **In the beginning, establish a safe place,** somewhere you go to when you are overwhelmed by emotions or intrusive thoughts. Recall an experience when you felt the most safe, secure, confident, at ease, at peace or comfortable. Visualize the environment and circumstances as vividly as possible. How old were you then? What are the colors, scenery, people, smells, etc. that are involved, and what is the context? How do you feel? Recall the situation vividly and abide in it for a while, allowing the feeling of safety, confidence or peace to arise and envelope you. Now tell yourself that whenever you

are overwhelmed with emotions and overtaken by pain and distress, you will recall the experience of this place. Transport yourself to that safe place and remain there for a while.

Since you are in the initial stages of familiarizing yourself with the practice, please choose a lightweight negative trait or cause of affliction, the opposite of which you would like to cultivate. Such a choice means avoiding, for the time being, engaging in and recalling intensely distressing or traumatic events or compulsive patterns of behavior. By "lightweight," I mean choose and concentrate, for example, on events of misunderstanding in which you were annoyed or frustrated but not furious or violent, or events in which you have displayed judgmental attitude or were subjected to such an attitude but not condemnation or disapproval.

2. **Concerning events that have already occurred:** recall and visualize a recent situation in which you had negative thoughts about causes of affliction and displayed their results, the opposite of which you would like to cultivate. Start by visualizing the environment in which the situation unfolded and took place, the people involved, the colors, the smells, etc. Such visualization should be as vivid as possible. Connect with the emerging emotions and thoughts along with the visualized mental pictures, observe them, and examine their results and how they are expressed or manifested within the circumstances.

   Now observe what the consequences are for you. How do you feel? Give it a name, a label. Keep yourself honest; do not become defensive or self-justifying in your thoughts and actions. Do not seek to compensate for those emotions or evade them.

   Now look at the face of the people involved. See how they show their presence to us through their faces and invoke our sense of responsibility toward the situation. The "face" is a metaphor for how one exposes his fragile and bare presence to us. The vulnerable face of the other is a mirror that tells us "no." Attending such a call is the ethics underlying the yogic practice of the opposites.

Examine their facial expressions and body language. What do you think they feel? How have your behavior and thoughts affected them? How do the consequences of your thoughts and their concrete results affect your connection with the other people involved? How do you feel when you see their faces? Can you drop your intense feelings for a while? How can you avoid repeating such a painful event? Cultivate empathy for the other and yourself, and generate a feeling of remorse and the strong wish not to repeat such behavior.

3. **Concerning events that are about to occur:** recall the negative thoughts or the results you have chosen to concentrate on and cultivate their opposites. Visualize similar events that may take place in the future that would revolve around your negative thoughts or their results. Visualize possible situations which did not happen yet, but that would trigger and stir those negative emotions, thoughts, and their consequences.

   Now observe: What are the consequences of such a situation for you? What do you feel? What are the implications of your emotions, thoughts and actions? Then, shifting your gaze, observe the face of the others involved, their expressions and body language, and ask yourself, what would they feel? How would your behavior and thoughts affect them? How would such an interaction look like in five or ten years from now? Would you continue to behave in the same manner? What would be the consequences of such a behavior? What would their faces mirror back to you then?

   Now that you are seeing the future and the possible dark consequences, please stop acting out of your causes of affliction and generate empathy by putting yourself in the others' shoes, and feel the relief associated with the decision not to repeat such behavior.

   At the same time, remain in that visualization in your open mental space, vacant of negative emotions, thoughts and interactions, and generate the opposite. In that visualized scene of the future, see yourself displaying vividly what you find to be the most appropriate ways of thinking and behaving.

Again, observe your feelings and look at the faces of the others involved in the interaction. How do you feel?

Cultivating the Opposite, Meeting the Opposite

So far, the practice of the opposite has been explored as a double practice, applied step by step. On the one hand, the yoga practitioner inquires about and examines the motives for thinking and behaving that violate the moral principles of yoga. On the other, he meditates upon their opposite while he reflects on the consequences of these thoughts and behaviors in light of self-honesty, sensitivity to others, and remorse through the use of imagination.

From Sūtra 2.48: "Then [the yogi] is not affected by opposites [or dualities, *dvandvas*]." [19] It is clear that a yogic physical posture depends on the practitioner's mental state. In other words, the practitioner may be absorbed in a stable and comfortable posture, consisting of a fine equilibrium of effort, relaxation and concentration, and remain in that posture as long as his mind is calm. After all, a mind that fluctuates without restraint, jumping from one thought to the next, cannot sustain such an ideal posture. A mind will become peaceful only when it is not dominated by pairs of opposites as the consequences of the *kleśas*, which are the causes of affliction and generators of mental fluctuations. Hence, the following verse referring to physical posture also applies to mental posture: "*Āsana* [yogic posture] is comfortably stable."[20] The method of merging the opposites, or the encounter with the opposite, is based on such a mental posture. It is a method derived from Patañjali's approach to the practice of the opposite, in which the practitioner does not depend on the pairs of opposites. It is intended not only to cultivate and adopt the opposite of a negative mental or emotional state, but also to lead to a situation in which the pairs of opposites no longer control or dominate the practitioner.

As discussed in Chapter 1, the causes of affliction (*kleśas*)—rejection or aversion *(dveṣa)* and attraction or acceptance (*rāga*)—always arise together, since they are pairs of opposites. The pain they inflict will endure as long as the practitioner has not cultivated the opposite of the inflicted pain or transcended its influence. In other words, every time a feeling, emotion or thought arises in his mind, the opposite immediately arises. They are inseparable, for pain does not exist without pleasure and confrontation does not exist without peace. When we experience a pair of opposites, such as deep sorrow and joy or shrinking shame and an intense sense of power, we remain trapped in the experience without being able to move forward. For example, experiencing pleasure implies a conscious or unconscious fear of losing it or of not being able to replicate it. The greater the importance of the experience of certain pleasure, the more we will fear its loss. However, it is possible to free ourselves from an oppressive conditioning influence if we experience the entire range of a certain pair of opposites. This kind of experiential understanding brings about the integration of the opposites, which is essential to opening up to the full experience of each of the opposites without being governed or dominated by them. In other words, one can contain both without being triggered or driven to act them out. Integration takes place when the practitioner stops trying to struggle with, or free himself from, a certain sensation, emotion or thought linked to one of the opposites.

Meeting with the opposite is a practice performed in meditation in which a practitioner generates a painful experience, including the sensations, emotions and thoughts associated with it. This act causes his painful experience to resurface, exposing his defense mechanisms. At the same time, insights may arise with regard to patterns of self-sabotage; for example, in events in which the practitioner inadvertently impairs himself in order to avoid confronting mental imprints that are threatening, overwhelming or embarrassing.

When these mental materials surface, their opposites surface simultaneously. As the integration between the two opposites deepens and progresses, the practitioner can stop identifying with the content of the painful experience, and he is able to increasingly establish a calm state of mind. The next stage of this meditation practice attempts to continue to sustain the calm state without being distracted, enabling real healing to take place when the pairs of opposites complement each other. In this meditation practice, the practitioner understands that in order to be free of pain, fear, anger or shame, and to experience peace and equanimity, he does not need to change circumstances or modify experiences, but rather to maintain a balance between the pairs of opposites.

Let's consider the following case study. Vanessa describes the emotions she experienced after separating from her partner, which stemmed from a fear of loss, abandonment, and never finding true love again. When we sat in meditation, I asked her to recall and generate that feeling of fear by first locating the place in the body where she felt it, and then looking into any images that arose in conjunction with the fear and describing them, all without trying to understand their implications. I asked her to find feelings that were opposite to the experience of fear. She remembered many events, seeing them vividly in her mind, in which she displayed courage that motivated her to initiate and complete projects while taking risks and maintaining her sense of vitality and strength.

Then I asked her to focus on the sense of courage that suffused her and place it on her body exactly where she had previously felt the fear. At that point I encouraged her to be curious and to watch what happened when the two emotions, fear and courage, were placed on one point. Vanessa reported that although the sharp sense of fear had diminished, become round and less threatening, she still felt its unpleasant presence. I asked her to focus again on the experience of pain and then to focus on the experiences of courage and to place them on the point where she had felt the fear. She repeated the process several times, alternately experiencing pain and courage, and then simultaneously experiencing them integrated in one physical spot. Eventually the pain subsided and became increasingly bearable, giving way to a burst of fresh energy and inner strength.

Vanessa's case shows us that she underwent a process of healing. Her fear lost its conditioning, threatening effect. However, the case is specific, related to a point in time, and it is impossible to know whether it had a long-term effect. But it testifies to an effective method in which the merging opposites are based on a mental posture. This method is implicit in the practice of the opposite and is derived from it. It is based on cultivating and adopting an opposite to a negative mental or emotional state through an encounter with the opposite, leading to a situation where pairs of opposites no longer control the practitioner.

4

Western Psychology as a Temporary Complement to Yoga

Reviewing the Practice of the Psychological Opposite

The yoga practitioner may encounter difficulties when engaging the practice of the psychological opposite aimed at stubborn and solid *kleśas* that require a long time to dismantle. Different levels of intensity associated with the causes of affliction are described in *Sūtra* 2.34: "To cultivate the opposite is [to reflect upon the fact] that thoughts which contradict the *yamas*, such as violent thoughts and so on ... whether mild, moderate, or intense, result in endless suffering [*duḥkha*] and ignorance [*ajñāna*]." The practice of the opposite, based on repetitive meditation (*abhyāsa*) and dispassionate and uninvolved awareness (*vairāgya*)—two complementary opposites—will alleviate suffering and bring it to an end, but it is difficult to implement and takes continuous effort applied over a long period of time.[1] The time needed to establish such an in-depth practice is mentioned in the Bhagavad Gītā, indicating that a yogi will attain the ultimate goal only after practicing yoga with restraint and effort for several lifetimes.[2] Ramana Maharshi (1879–1950),[3] one of the most prominent teachers of the last century, also said that this practice is very long. It requires constant, uninterrupted training, as the mind is accustomed to objectification; that is, it obsessively identifies and labels objects of perception, whether desiring them or avoiding them. The mind finds it difficult to shift the focus of its attention inward and become collected and composed.

Practicing the opposite is a lengthy practice, for ultimate yoga is a meditative state, independent of the concealed and latent mental imprints, whether they promote silence or stillness of mind or serve as a seedbed for pain and suffering. Only then is the practitioner of yoga able to abide in the true Self and be free from these imprints; that is, from the roots of the causes of affliction. Until then, the yogi has to cultivate mental imprints that induce peace and silence (*saṃskāras* of the *nirodha* type). He will do so by meditating or practicing the psychological opposite until mental imprints of stillness will dominate the ones that bear pain and suffering (*saṃskāras* of the *vyutthāna* type). Only when the mental imprints that bear pain and suffering are dissolved, obstructed or silenced will the mind become imperturbable, allowing the practitioner to experience an increasing sense of relief. Yoga practice solidifies and thickens the layer of mental imprints that still the mind so that it can become more peaceful for longer periods of time. But what will the yoga practitioner do until then with the patterns of behavior that repeatedly cause pain and harm to himself and his surroundings? How will he conduct himself in the face of patterns that prevent him from moving toward personal growth, toward a harmonious relationship with his family, friends and community, and the realization of yoga?

On the face of it, the ideal method for dealing with the *saṃskāras* is the direct method that Patañjali mentions: "Through sākṣāt-karaṇa [direct yogic perception] of the *saṃskāras*, knowledge of previous births is obtained."[4] The opening of the *Sūtra* is intriguing. In the psychological context, the capacity to look directly into the *saṃskāras* suggests an immediate and profound understanding of the root causes of affliction, along with an understanding of how they were created. Conceptualizations or judgments cannot disclose this deep immediate understanding; it is independent of one's beliefs and perceptions. It dawns as a stroke of insight, comprehended all at once as a complete picture. Direct reflection enables the unconscious to surface and become conscious. Thus, instead of coping with the symptoms of mental imprints by avoidance, for example, such insights make it possible to identify, disempower, and dissolve the mental imprints directly.

Most of the *Yoga Sūtras*' commentators interpreted this verse in the context of the third chapter of the text, which refers to the extraordinary forces and abilities the yogi acquires in the course of his deepening, determined and persistent training. But Mehta[5] goes one step further and provides a commentary on the *Sūtra* from a psychological perspective. For him, a yogi is able to directly perceive and identify mental imprints, not because of a particular set of circumstances or stimuli, but because the defense mechanisms that usually conceal the mental imprints are suspended. The direct perception of mental imprints enables the yogi to see them without a screen of explanations—without protection, without justification and without refutation—but with a clear awareness that they are only fluctuations or mental processes stirring in one's mind.

Deep concentration, or meditative absorption, a state of mind occupied by one object (in this case one mental imprint), allows the yogi to know his past. He can understand his reactions to past events that were etched in his mind as mental imprints at the time of the incident. If a yogi gains insight into the manner in which a certain mental imprint was formed, that mental imprint will instantly lose its potential to cause him to act it out. Mehta correctly notes that the active dimension of past events continues to exist within one's present thoughts and behaviors; the past is enfolded within the present. Consequently, the past can be traced, detected and understood by observing patterns of behavior, habits, tendencies and reactions in the present. Direct observation, without the mediation of concepts and explanations, reveals the roots of past events. Adopting such an approach would mean that the supernatural power mentioned in the above *Sūtra* is nothing more than a direct method that may help the yoga practitioner to silence his thoughts and emotions and deepen his yoga practice.

However, it takes a long time to cultivate and refine such a direct method and to acquire sufficient skill to employ it. In his book *After the Ecstasy, the Laundry*, author and *vipassanā* teacher Jack Kornfield described the experiences of yoga practitioners who devoted many years to meditative and spiritual work with teachers in India. They stated that their deep experiences of meditation had positive results, such as long periods of silence and a growing sense of compassion. But they also described experiences of emotional crises, including feelings of emptiness and meaninglessness, addiction or tremendous regression in their self-esteem. In other words, despite reaching heightened spiritual experiences through the skills they acquired in yoga and meditation, their mental imprints persisted as subterranean currents, ready at any moment, in the face of any stimulus, to activate a cause of affliction.

Kornfield relates that one of the practitioners, an American yoga and meditation teacher, discovered freedom after twenty years of spiritual search while training with a guru in India. He reported that he had experienced continuous perfection and was abiding in stillness and love. After his stay in India, he returned to the United States with his pregnant wife. In the next two years, groups of practitioners began to gather around him, practicing meditation every day under his guidance. On the face of it, he seemed to have managed to transcend the problems and stresses of mundane existence. But then, there was a turbulent crisis in his life:

> But then it happened to me. I received a crash course in confusion, panic and depression. It all started when I became very sick with leftover parasites from India. Then all the money I had saved for years and invested in two thriving businesses was lost through bankruptcy and betrayal. All of a sudden, the "guru" was sick and poor. I became terribly frightened. My family life became a place of conflict. We had to leave our home, to struggle with money, to worry about ordinary things. I had difficulty with my mother. And all the while I thought I should not be feeling these things—I'd been to the peaks, after all. I thought I knew the whole game. Finally, I had to stop teaching. I lost all control. I had reached a childish stage where I wasn't trying to understand things; I was just broken completely, living moment to moment, and in some way that's when my spiritual life really became genuine for the first time.[6]

It seems that the practitioner had to stay with his guru longer and practice silence and compassion continuously and consistently. He was supposed to do so in an environment devoid of stimuli, since the stimuli could ignite and trigger the *saṃskāras*, which seemed to be very volatile. It is possible that the departure from the original practice environment in India, the return to the United States, and the disease, exposed the latent mental imprints to a network of stimuli, a psychological network that had not been attended to. These stimuli triggered mental imprints and created a series of painful and shattering situations reflected in the patterns of behavior associated with the causes of affliction.

As this case would suggest, it appears that when the practice of the psychological opposite only includes its meditative aspects it will be limited to a cognitive strategy, since it is not directed toward the root of causes of affliction. It may be effective for coping with relatively weak causes of affliction, and possibly also with those that are of moderate intensity. Its effectiveness will depend on the yoga practitioner's determination, capacity and skills.

Furthermore, unresolved psychological matters can also be noticeable in those perceived by others as contemporary "accomplished yogis" (or self-proclaimed "accomplished yogis"). These may be masked as "crazy wisdom" yogis, justifying antinomianism, which rejects laws or legalism and argues against moral, religious or social norms, while still being driven by their shadows.

The "shadow," from a psychological perspective, refers to the unconscious aspect of the personality that the conscious does not identify in itself. As such it is unknown.

Jung argues that the shadow includes everything outside the range of consciousness which may be positive or negative. He continues: "and the less it is embodied in the individual's conscious life, the blacker and denser it is."[7] As such it is subjected to various defense mechanisms, by which what one denies for oneself is projected onto the other. In the context of the psychology of yoga, the shadow might stand for the layer of *saṃskāras*, the latent and concealed mental imprints, and these projections might stand as a mental wall of ignorance between one's sense of I-am-ness and the real Self.

Found in all the major religions of the world, "crazy wisdom" as a concept is mostly associated with the Tibetan tradition, and refers to a unique and unusual mode of spiritual teaching in action that aims to constantly challenge the students' beliefs, and confront them with the naked truth of existence. Accordingly, accomplished yogis use unconventional means that seem crazy, offensive, outrageous or unexpected in the eyes of others, and are designed to shock and lead one out of one's fences of personality.

Such an accomplished yogi is said to be acting spontaneously, or "naturally," out of their spiritual accomplishment, in a manner not filtered or mediated by the yogi's ego-personality, because such a yogi has transcended his ego. In other words, he acts from pure awareness. Such "pure" conduct should be carefully distinguished from mere impulsive, emotional or abusive behavior.

Here is the testimony of artist and former nun Damcho Dyson, who was hurt, if not traumatized, by the so-called "crazy wisdom" demonstrated by the acclaimed contemporary Tibetan teacher and author Sogyal Rinpoche (1947–2019). It points out that what was supposed to be the practice of "crazy wisdom" was but abusive behavior:

> The few who openly questioned Sogyal's manner of teaching were made an example of through a publicly humiliating dialogue that could completely hijack a teaching session. We were told by Sogyal and his senior students that these so-called training sessions were "activity teachings" and Sogyal's erratic and tantrum-like behavior was "crazy wisdom," and the way to view it correctly was to cultivate "pure perception." ... the frequency and severity of private beatings and public humiliations increased. For many of us in the "inner circle" it was not uncommon to have multiple lumps on our skulls or split scalps from beating. He once ripped my ear. We all saw that his worst moods were caused by problems with the young attractive females—students he'd groomed for sexual relationships—that were on call to him 24/7. Only later was I to hear from some of them personally that they had been raped. They had been coerced into the relationship by being told they were engaging in consort practice, *karmamudra*."[8]

One's inability to perceive Sogyal's actions as stemming from crazy wisdom and compassion would mean that one lacked "pure perception," enabling one to discern between crazy acts of compassion and illegal and amoral activities. The "discerning disciple" would claim that Sogyal's crazy-wisdom act was a means of awakening him out of his ignorance and the grip of the ego. This criterion of pure perception was used to justify Sogyal's activities, which were supposed to be beyond law and religious or social norms, while in fact being abuse driven by Sogyal's shadow.

Feuerstein dedicated his work *Holy Madness: The Shock Tactics and Radical Teachings of Crazy-Wise Adepts, Holy Fools and Rascal Gurus* to the phenomenon of "crazy wisdom," or "holy madness," exploring first-hand accounts of accomplished modern teachers or yogis, such as Rajneesh and Chögyam Trungpa, and of their students, who were hurt by their teachers' crazy-wise excesses. He argues that those who are said to be fully awakened may still have some work to do on their psychology.[9] Such teachers are oriented toward transcending their sense of I-am-ness (ego), instead of toward self-fulfillment, or the realization of their psychic wholeness, which is based on the integration of the shadow into consciousness. Such teachers tend to see psychic wholeness a by-product of ego transcendence, while integration is a lifelong process that involves an intentional change in one's psychic wholeness that is visible to others. If integration is not a conscious program of the one-after-enlightenment, it will be very difficult to form such an integration due to unresolved psychic structures. In the absence of such integration, the peculiar eccentricity of the enlightened adepts who teach in the style of "crazy wisdom" can become potentially dangerous. The danger is that their messages that stem from "crazy wisdom" are filtered through their shadow.

In the short term, even a skillful and resourceful yoga practitioner may be distressed when his life is collapsing, as we saw in Kornfield's example, or haunted by his shadow, as we saw in the case of Sogyal. What would this yogi be required to do in order to get rid of the compulsive causes of affliction whose intensity was so high? Is he destined to continue to be subject to the power of such mental imprints? Should he trust the process he is going through and hope that the karma will enable new possibilities and outcomes? Should he continue to practice the opposite, with the expectation that the reservoir of mental imprints that bring about stillness will ultimately overcome the imprints that bear pain and suffering?

Practicing the opposite intended for a medium- or high-intensity *kleśa* may also cause deception associated with the sense of I-am-ness, like the thinking that seeks to excuse a certain behavior resulting from anger or jealousy, or the pride and sense of power that accompany success after temporarily overcoming a *kleśa*, or experiencing humiliation and a sense of defeat after acting out of a cause of affliction. These feelings may create an obstacle that would make it difficult to recognize the ego and acknowledge its characteristics, such as vanity, shame, righteousness and guilt. Even if a yoga practitioner wants to examine the roots of the problem; that is, to identify and treat the mental imprints, it is likely that he will find it difficult, because they are latent, hidden deep within his personality.

In order to illustrate the difficulty of cultivating the opposite of any *kleśa*, either of weak, medium or high intensity, we can imagine the ocean's waves breaking one after the other on a rock. First the wave washes over the dry sand. Next the waves break on the rock one after the other, more frequently and for a longer period of time, until they dissolve the dry mud that clings to the rock and wash it off. They then begin to erode small particles from the rock itself. The waves are the repetitive meditation cultivating the opposite. The sand, the mud and the rock are the causes of affliction in their three intensities. When a yoga practitioner's emotions are as strong as a rock and impose pain and suffering upon himself and his environment, what will he do? According to the practice of the opposite it would take a long time to erode and dismantle the emotions' charge, conditioning power and contents. How then will the practitioner dissolve such a difficult emotional burden?

This series of questions examines the effectiveness of the silence and compassion of meditation against reality. It teaches us that the ability of the practice to alleviate the suffering of man in the phenomenal world is limited in the short term. It would seem that the most important arena for understanding the causes of affliction is in the realm of emotions associated with intimate relationships. Again, it must be noted that yoga practice and meditation may be spiritual bypasses or evasive movements away from the real and direct confrontation with feelings, relationships and the demands of phenomenal existence.

Western Psychology and Mental Imprints

Psychology emerged as a scientific framework in the second half of the nineteenth century and was associated with physiologist Wilhelm Wundt (1832–1920), who established the psychological laboratory in Leipzig University which brought experimental psychology to the world. This framework was different from neurobiology and philosophy, and had the intent of understanding and explaining the mind, feelings, and what motivates human behavior. During the nineteenth and twentieth centuries, different schools of psychology developed that represented the major theories within psychology: behaviorism, gestalt, humanism, psychoanalysis and cognitive. These schools of thoughts became the source of many psychological areas of study, and their therapeutic processes developed as reactions to one another. For example, the school of cognitive psychology covers the study of mental processes including how people think, perceive, remember and learn, and is related to other disciplines, including neuroscience, philosophy and linguistics. It emerged as a reaction to behaviorism that seemed to fail to account for how internal processes impact behavior. The main criticism of cognitive psychology is that it is not directly observable. For example, memories cannot be directly observed. The retrieval of memories and reexperiencing them in a therapy session is a relevant and essential theme to the therapy of mental imprints.

Another example concerns the school of humanistic psychology that had developed as a response to psychoanalysis and behaviorism focusing on individual choices, personal growth and realizing one's potential. While psychoanalysis and behaviorism schools of thought primarily addressed negative or abnormal human behavior, humanistic psychology differed considerably by its emphasis on helping people achieve and fulfill their potential.[10]

Other important developments in the study of psychology concern neuroscience studies and trauma-informed approaches. Both have gained currency recently, and so are worth mentioning. Neuropsychology is a branch of psychology that is concerned with how the brain's and the nervous system's conditions affect one's psychology in terms of cognitive function and behavior. For example, *The Nature* reported that major depression may often be caused by two genes that regulate the activity of glutamate, a neurotransmitter that is released by nerve cells in the brain.[11] Neuropsychology aims at discovering the way the brain corresponds with the mind. It is a relatively new discipline within the field of psychology. Although the history of its development can be traced back to the Third Dynasty in Ancient Egypt,[12] the first textbook defining the field, *Fundamentals of Human Neuropsychology*, was initially published by Kolb and Whishaw in 1980.[13] Clinical neuropsychology has clearly proliferated as a diagnostic discipline; however, as Ruff argues,[14] patients' needs are not met by merely diagnosing cognitive deficits, as there is a growing need to advance services that maintain cognitive health.

Trauma-informed approaches include strategies for screening to identify those persons who have been exposed to life-threatening trauma and impacted by symptoms of PTSD, and then get them the appropriate treatment. Trauma-informed approaches further aim at integrating knowledge about trauma into policies, procedures and practices seeking to actively resist retraumatization, and to inform implementation and sustainment of trauma-informed care across the individual patient encounter to health systems and communities at large.[15]

But how does one infuse a trauma-informed approach through a whole society (including its cultural, historical and gender issues), while encouraging safety, trustworthiness and transparency, along with peer support, collaboration and mutuality? By guiding legislation and public policy, thereby reshaping cities? There are so many interests that could be involved in this, such as political ones, and this may include the desire to get funding for their causes, or the phenomenon that humans need someone or something to blame when things go wrong.[16]

Regarding psychology frameworks of the West and of yoga, I would like to briefly talk about the work of two scholars who contributed to the research on yoga and psychology: Harold Coward and Georg Feuerstein. Coward has attempted in his meticulous work *Yoga and Psychology: Language, Memory, and Mysticism* to compare yoga and Western psychology, exploring mostly the parallel notions of karma, its residues as *saṃskāras vāsanās*, and *kleśas*, memory, and the limits of human nature according to Western psychanalysts Freud and Jung, and, according to the yogic potential, to transcend such limits of the sense of I-am-ness. In his exploration of the questions of the limits of human nature, he extends his comparison to Western transpersonal psychology, examining categories of transpersonal experience. These include detailed controversies between philosophers and psychologists, such as Michael Washburn and Ken Wilber, but Abraham Maslow's voice is not represented. Although Coward's book laid important foundations for the comparative study of yoga and Western psychology, he based his comparison mostly on the psychoanalysis theories of Freud and Jung, without questioning their relevance to modern methodology and the use of psychoanalysis and psychotherapy. He proceeds to discuss the transpersonal-psychology theories of Washburn, Wilber and John Hick, while Western psychology, as shown earlier in an anecdotal manner, includes other schools of thought and therapy, such as behaviorism, gestalt, cognitive, neuropsychology and trauma-informed approaches and therapies, the consideration of which could inform a wider frame of comparison and understanding. In all probability, the scope of extending such a comparison is too wide and would require a separate research project that may concern areas such as parapsychology and yogic super-natural powers (*siddhis*), therapeutic somatic methods and the yogic postures, and the role of the psychologist along with the role of teacher/guru.

Despite the possible debate about the possibility for the one standard of epistemology concerning the limits of human nature (which could be applied to both systems), and as I suggest that there is one standard as a spectrum on which each system can be located or positioned (but with a different epistemic horizon), I tend to agree with Coward. He concludes his work by stating that with regard to the limits of human nature: "a good comparative scholarship requires that we examine such claims from within the presuppositions of their own world views."[17] In such a state of affairs, both systems can still inform each other—the understanding of one may be enhanced by contrasting it with the other, or by both being complementary.

Feuerstein, in his work *The Psychology of Yoga*,[18] sought to present a combination of psychological approaches from the East and the West to achieve a deeper understanding of the mind. He studied various schools of psychology focusing on the mind, ego, behavior, sensations, perceptions, emotions and consciousness. He believed that the schools closest to yoga are those that adopt a humanistic and values-based vision and provide a "transpersonal consciousness model."[19] His reference was the humanistic psychology developed by American psychologist Abraham

Maslow (1909–1970).[20] Humanistic psychology seeks to create a comprehensive view regarding the meaning of human existence and illuminate aspects of human experience, such as love, compassion, hope and creativity. Transpersonal psychology, based on humanistic psychology, began to develop in the 1960s. Its basic assumption is that the human psyche or mind is capable of developing beyond man's personality through spiritual experiences in which the mind extends beyond the conventional boundaries of the ego, and beyond the limitations of time and space.

In the past, psychologists often identified themselves exclusively with one single school of thought. Today, most psychologists have an eclectic outlook on psychology. They often draw on ideas and theories from different schools rather than holding to any singular perspective.[21] Thus, there are streams of Western psychology that can offer a wide range of methods for dealing with the difficulties in cultivating the opposite, a process that would require a long, ongoing, reflective effort and understanding that mediation may be a spiritual bypass, an evasive movement, away from the real and direct confrontation with feelings, relationships, and the demands of phenomenal existence. This is complementary to the yogic practice of the opposite. It may provide an appropriate response for the yoga practitioner who suffers from persistent and intense suffering from a particular cause of affliction.

However, I do not propose merging or integrating here the yogic practice of the opposite with Western psychology, given its complex thought, debates of various schools, criticisms regarding the differences among various streams of psychological theories and the wide range of therapeutic methods they offer. That would require in-depth comparative research in order to find the common ground and hermeneutics for each approach so as to bridge the conceptual divides of time, place and culture. I do not seek to merge methods of East and West, as in many cases integration may dilute the essence of yoga in its broad meaning as a path to liberation consistent with ancient meaning of Dharma as the holistic "right way to live": following one's duties, rituals, rights, laws, conduct and virtues. Although it is known, for example, that the integration of mindfulness meditation in Western cognitive psychology has had positive effects for treatment, such integration is still addressing a specific matter. Furthermore, to mix the two would imply that the Dharma is lacking in methods to really help people, as if one were to say that the Dharma needs adjustment or improvement that would be provided by Western psychology. In this case, however, the question of integrating the two disciplines is a complex one. My goal here is to offer the yoga practitioner who is addressing a specific psychological problem access to complementary Western psychological methods after he has exhausted the psychological method of yoga.

It is impossible to speak of these two approaches without noting, at least in general, the similarities and differences between them. The approaches of yoga and Western psychology share the fundamental understanding that suffering is a characteristic of the human existence, and it is possible and desirable to treat it. Both methods attempt to trace the causes of suffering through an inner journey to the depths of the self through the process of healing. Selfhood, with its conscious and unconscious layers, is the focus of the two disciplines. However, each approach has a different perception of Selfhood. In the West, Selfhood is based on the concept of individualism and individual sovereignty. Its existence does not depend on the fulfillment of a traditional agenda dictated by an external source, such as the family, society or a religious institution. The identity of the individual is based on one's skills, one's talents, and on the realization of one's potential. Yoga, on the other hand, is not based on individualism. At the top of the list of priorities lies the true Self (*puruṣa*), which is independent of the body, emotions, feelings, thoughts, and family and social belonging, and is beyond the goal of realizing the potential of the individual. Western psychology, with its varied schools of thought, enables a deep understanding of the individual mind and its development from childhood to adulthood. It allows us to understand how internal conflicts are created, why they recur, and what their defense mechanisms and inherent dynamics are. Psychological healing takes place through the understanding and clarification of these aspects and by working with the individual's internal dynamics. In other words, while the psychology of yoga casts the spotlight on the real and unconditioned Self which is independent of place and time, Western psychology focuses on the conditioned self, which is subject to internal dynamics and its development over time.

The purpose of both disciplines is also not the same. Western psychology seeks to reduce suffering as much as possible and improve one's condition in phenomenal existence. Patañjali's yoga, on the other hand, seeks to extricate one from the cycle of birth and death and from phenomenal existence, and to release one completely from suffering into a supernatural state while stilling one's mind, a stillness that is contrary to mental processes and mundane activities stemming from *avidyā*. Psychology seeks to process mental content, whose roots are in events and memories that have left their mark, while yoga seeks to neutralize and empty one's mind of these contents in order to silence it, releasing one from the grip of mental imprints and the resulting causes of affliction.

In addition, the *Yoga Sūtras* rarely address feelings, to the point of almost ignoring them altogether. In Western psychology, emotions are the main object of inquiry into one's psyche. It is that tension that motivated me to explore the psychology of yoga and to identify it as a psychological method that forms an essential new layer to the many existing layers of interpretation of the *Yoga Sūtras*, both classical and modern, and to the practice of yoga.

Another difference that has motivated me to develop a psychotherapeutic yogic method stems from the difficulties in practicing the opposite, as well as difficulties in dealing with intimate relationships and their emotional complexity. The roots of the difficulties are directly linked to the latent mental imprints. Because they are concealed and deep in the mind, their identification and recognition are a great challenge to yogis. In his meditation, the yogi carries a dual role: he observes his mind with the aim of bringing it to stillness, but at the same time he carries its contents and hidden roots. I believe that this double role has a weakness, for the attempt to silence the agitated, distracted, active mind by means of mental activity is a kind of closed circuit from which it is almost impossible to extricate oneself. Achieving such a goal takes a long time, even lifetimes.

It can be said that the role of the teacher is to place a mirror in front of the student to reflect his habitual tendencies and to assist him in the process of healing his psyche. It is surprising, however, that in the *Yoga Sūtras*, the guru-teacher's role is not mentioned directly, and only in the context of the concept of *Īśvara*, the lord or deity who is the teacher of all the devoted yogis.[22] On this point I agree with Raveh, who states that one can clearly understand from the *Yoga Sūtras* that the guru is not completely necessary for the fulfillment of yoga, and the responsibility for its realization rests mainly with the practitioner and his sense of responsibility and determination.[23]

In his commentary to *Sūtra* 3.6, and his interpretation of the stages leading to implementation of the *Saṃyama* type of meditation,[24] Vyāsa asserts, "Yoga is to be known by yoga, and yoga itself leads to yoga. He who remains steadfast in yoga always delights in it."[25] That is to say, yoga itself is the teacher. It guides the practitioner and he can understand from it when to proceed and make progress to the next stage. However, it is his responsibility to initiate a move to the next stage, stemming from his understanding and experience of a given stage of yoga.

It is important to emphasize this aspect of personal responsibility, especially in view of the growing phenomenon in India and the West in which charismatic gurus, who are perceived as spiritually enlightened and in possession of special forces, gather around them communities of disciples and followers. Disciples often tend to suspend their sense of autonomy and place their trust in the teachers in the hope that they will find immediate solutions to their personal problems. This assertion is not meant to argue against the necessity or the importance of a guru on the journey toward the realization of yoga, but to stress the personal responsibility of the practitioner in his journey. He needs to pay attention to the difficulties of practicing the opposite in the short term when dealing with intimate relationships, including intimate relationships with yoga teachers and the emotions involved. The emphasis on personal responsibility opens a window onto Western psychology and allows us to see it as a complementary option, as it offers a wide range of methods for dealing with hidden or latent mental imprints.

Dismantling Mental Imprints in Western Psychology

One of the areas that Western psychologic methods have addressed effectively is the problem of compulsive disorders. Levels of compulsion in behavior patterns can be associated with the intensity levels of the *kleśas*, as outlined by Patañjali. Compulsion levels may also lead to impulsive disorders.

The method I have chosen to present here is but one of many methods included in psychotherapy, and this choice does not constitute a recommendation for it or a declaration of its superiority over other methods. It is important to make this clear, because of the debates and criticisms that exist regarding the differences among various psychological theories, their application, and their therapeutic effectiveness.

The method I have selected demonstrates how to cope with situations involving stress, anxiety and compulsive behavior using the language of modern psychology. In this method one can clearly identify the mental imprints, the patterns of behavior, and the causes of the affliction. One can understand how this method can assist the yoga practitioner in dismantling the emotional burden associated with high-intensity causes of affliction. The method deals with compulsive-impulsive disorders that cause tremendous suffering, and is based on a method developed by American psychologist Francine Shapiro (1948–2019): eye movement desensitization and reprocessing (EMDR). My point of departure is the relationship between the intensity levels of *kleśas* already mentioned by Patañjali and the compulsive levels of habitual tendencies. Shapiro's method is based on eye movements. The patient is asked to visually follow the movements of the therapist's finger, moving in random directions with no specific pattern while recalling disturbing memories.[26] The concentration required to follow these movements reduces the patient's sensitivity, pacifies the inundation of emotions, and weakens the defense mechanisms. It places the patient in a position of observation that prevents him from drowning in the painful scenes that are projected in his mind while he experiences them again. Thus, the patient can recall the memory of an event that left its mark on his psyche, and he is now able to process it for the first time.

This therapy addresses memories that were not processed because of a person's inability to contain the intensity of the pain it caused, a memory that remained frozen in time with all the sights, sounds, smells, feelings and emotions associated with it. Such a memory is difficult to access, as it may expose the person to the painful or traumatic experience all over again. In her book, Shapiro describes how she discovered that eye movements can reduce anxiety when they are moving in all directions and at different speeds.

She elaborates on how she has incorporated prominent elements of key schools of psychology into her method.[27] Her book is full of testimonies. For example, during one of the sessions in which a patient practiced eye movements, Shapiro asked the patient to focus on an obsessive thought that made her anxious. The anxiety stemmed from a quarrel she had had with her neighbor, and Shapiro instructed her to allow the associations linked to the event—the images, emotions and physical sensations—to arise unobstructed in her mind without trying to influence or modify them. In this process, the memory of the quarrel with the neighbor was reworked, and the images and feelings associated with it began to change. After the patient accessed a neutral feeling about the event, the anxiety began to dissipate. She managed to capture the event as it really was instead of the way it had been colored by her anxiety, and at the end of the process the event became a distant memory. A renewed thought or recall of the event no longer aroused the old anxiety, and the patient's level of distress diminished considerably.

The method developed by American psychologist Robert Miller is based both on the principles of EMDR and the principles of treating impulsive and compulsive disorders.[28] In his view, obsessive compulsions are created when positive emotions about certain behaviors or objects create state-dependent memory. For example, if the feeling "I win" is related to the amassing of gambling profits, a compulsive addiction to gambling may develop. A memory of the event together with the feelings experienced forms a unit called a "feeling state," which is responsible for a pattern of compulsive behavior.[29]

The intensity of the emotion experienced during the event will shape the memory, rather than the quality of the emotion, whether positive or negative. The term "feeling" or "feeling state" does not apply only to emotions such as joy or anger, but to a complex range of feelings, emotions and thoughts. In an assertion such as "I feel strong," a person expresses a whole gamut of physical feelings and emotions associated with that thought. Compulsive behavior that develops from a feeling state is not limited to traumatic situations, but may also be related to drunken experiences, fears and psychophysiological conditions that lead to feelings such as excitement or joy that create state-dependent memories.[30]

For example, from a feeling state of "I win"—that is, the complex of emotions, sensations and thoughts that accompany the intoxicating memory of a gambling win—a compulsive addiction to gambling might ensue. It is important to understand that some behavior becomes negative only if it is compulsive. For example, shopping alone is not negative behavior. However, when a person identifies with a feeling state of "I have a high economic status" that is linked to shopping, compulsive consumerism may develop.

According to Miller, obsessive-compulsive disorder can be characterized by three types of internal beliefs. The first type is the negative belief, such as "I am a defeatist," which is at the base of a certain feeling state. These negative beliefs are hidden and camouflaged by positive emotions. Thus, emotions arising from success in a competitive race, for example, may be the result of their underlying feeling state, for a feeling that is essentially defeatist can motivate a person to prove the opposite. It is therefore difficult to identify such internal beliefs. A second type of inner belief is the seemingly positive one created by positive events. For example, a gambler may adhere to the belief "I win" after he has drawn huge profits. This is a positive belief embedded in the feeling state responsible for compulsive behavior. Finally, the third type is based on negative beliefs created by lack of self-control. For example, a person can develop the belief "I always complicate everything" because of difficulties created by his compulsive gambling addiction.

Miller presents the case of John, a patient who suffered from compulsive behavior.[31] John was not interested in solving problems related to trauma or difficulties in childhood, or even events in adult life. Even when these problems surfaced during treatment, he refused to discuss them. It is precisely for this reason that the therapeutic encounter is interesting, for it was clearly demonstrated that Miller's therapeutic method was effective without the influence of other methods.

John was a successful thirty-five-year-old broker who had a long history of gambling problems. He lost over one million dollars playing poker over a ten-year period. Although he took part in anonymous rehabilitation groups for gambling addicts, he was unable to free himself from his compulsive behavior. As a result of gambling, he ran into debt and became depressed for long periods of time. He often won by playing cleverly, but in the end he always lost control, and the game. Even when he had the upper hand, he continued to play until he lost everything he had won.

In the first session, John recognized a feeling state. When asked to imagine a poker game, he described a feeling state of excitement because of the considerable gains he had imagined. He recalled exactly what hand he'd had in the game, and the memory was so vivid that his face became flushed with excitement. Miller instructed John to imagine such a poker game and practice eye movements simultaneously. After practicing three sets of eye movements, his level of excitement decreased. At the second meeting, John reported that he had been less involved in gambling during the past week, though he still felt a strong urge to play poker. He felt something had changed, since it was not as hard to leave the card table. In order to identify his feelings he was asked to reimagine a poker game, and after practicing three sets of eye movements, the thrill of the sense of winning dissipated completely.

In order to identify the negative beliefs associated with or underlying his feeling of winning, John was asked why winning was so important to him. He discovered that when he was a child his father called him a loser every time he was angry with him. This event had left its mark on John's psyche. He recognized that the negative belief at the base of the "I am winning" feeling is "I am nothing." In other words, the positive feeling state to which he had become addicted was based on a negative mental imprint, a *saṃskāra* that was etched in his psyche because of an event that had led to obsessive-compulsive behavior.

This pattern dictated the course of his life. He felt a strong urge to compensate and prove the opposite of the mental imprint or the negative feeling state; that is, he wanted to prove that he was not a loser. At the base of his compulsive behavior was an emotion of shame, a *dveṣa*, a cause of affliction that led to avoidance and rejection. The corrective affirmative belief that John cultivated was "I can succeed," a realistic and achievable reversal that might have freed him from shame.

Negative beliefs such as "I am helpless," "I am a loser," or "nothing changes the situation," are at the basis of the intense desire for an opposite positive feeling, such as "I am capable," or "I win." It is clear that a person who feels strong negative emotions may also feel strongly about their positive opposite in certain circumstances. Strong positive emotions may create a feeling state that results in a behavioral disturbance, because it is in itself a compulsive reaction that seeks to compensate for the negative feeling state.

The week after the second treatment, John did not even go to the club, and he said he thought of poker only a few times. But he returned the following week. He spent four hours there every night, but this time he focused on people rather on than winning or making money. During the treatment, he identified a sense of belonging to the group of card players. It represented a feeling state connecting the card game with the sense of social belonging. He even expressed the negative belief underlying the desire for camaraderie: "No one wants me." The emotion underlying this belief was fear. The positive affirmative belief that he cultivated was "I am accepted."

In the next two meetings, John identified his negative beliefs. After practicing a series of eye movements, the intensity of the feeling states diminished almost completely. Instead, John cultivated and internalized realistic positive beliefs, such as "I'm OK" and "sometimes I'm successful." Three months later, in a telephone follow-up interview, John reported that the obsession was not bothering him anymore. He said that his life was balanced, he enjoyed poker twice a week, and he was succeeding in his work and in his marriage.

It is surprising that the healing process, the dismantling of gambling compulsion, was not based on strategies of avoiding card games, such as keeping a few miles away from the club in order to avoid temptation, a strategy that characterizes cognitive-behavioral therapy. The process that John underwent allowed him to moderately enjoy card games out of choice without being in the grip of the compulsion of the game. In other words, the healing process led to a state of mind in which he neither avoided the card game nor was he addicted to it.

It should be noted that cognitive-behavioral therapy is often effective, as it allows the patient to control compulsive behavior. However, it does not process the feeling state that depends on the memory underlying the behavior, so sooner or later the compulsive behavior may again get out of control. The same is true of *Pratipakṣa bhāvanā*. The practitioner applies indirect methods to cultivate the opposite through the double practice, which helps to control compulsive behavior. But here too, the feeling state depends on the underlying memory remaining unprocessed. In other words, the practitioner does not attempt to identify the mental imprints that underlie the feeling state and to disassociate them from their activating power. The compulsive behavior may therefore get out of control once again.

It can be argued that cases such as John's are extreme and unusual, as they are concerned with traumatic and compulsive addiction, behaviors that do not seem to characterize most yoga practitioners. It is even possible to assume that such treatment is not necessary as long as one consistently practices the yogic *Pratipakṣa bhāvanā*. But the testimonies of practitioners quoted in Kornfield's book tell a different story. What emerges from these accounts is that, along with continuous states of mind of silence and compassion, practitioners have experienced emotional crises, addiction, and a tremendous regression in their self-esteem.

It is true that the theory of feeling states is suitable to extreme cases of trauma, addictions and anxiety, but as Miller claims, memory-dependent states are also present in other psychophysiological conditions. This teaches us that trauma is not the only experience that can cause a memory-dependent state of mind, and that psychophysiological states, which result from feelings such as excitement, joy or completeness, may produce state-dependent memories as well.

If so, yoga practitioners can use a practice that involves removing layers of hidden mental content that dictate and modulate their lives, while at the same time they can turn to certain Western-psychology methods as temporary and supplemental therapies. This applies not only to yoga practitioners, but also to religious devotees who are limited to religious and moral injunctions or to guidelines dictated by their religious way of life. They may use the methods of Western psychology if they fail to implement the commandments and moral principles of their religion, or in cases that cause suffering to themselves and others. However, since the manifesting causes of affliction imply an incapacity to implement the moral principles of either yoga or a given religion, we need to consider that psychology is not, and cannot be, a moral framework. That is its advantage, and that is also its limit. On the one hand, it puts into question old ethical rules, which are based on compliance with authority, scripture and tradition. For example, a woman comes to a psychologist. She does not know whether to divorce or stay in her safe but unsatisfying marriage. The psychologist will not advise her to put her selfish search for emotional thrills over her children's needs for stability and safety. He will seek an answer to her dilemma within their dialogue without judgment or the pretension of knowing the solution in advance. On the other hand, a psychologist who will listen to a man telling her about his marital infidelity and convey to her patient the moral discomfort and condemnation she feels will be seen as an unprofessional psychologist, or one that needs further training. Psychologists will not exercise moral judgment on us and will not preach morality. Without the non-verbal agreement that the psychologist-patient relationship does not include a reprimand for immorality, patients would not enter this relationship.

Nevertheless, the theme of removing layers of hidden mental content that dictates and modulates their lives, while at the same time turning to certain Western-psychology methods as a temporary complementary therapy, will be discussed further in chapter six. Based on the teachings of the fourteenth-century Tibetan Buddhist scholar and teacher Longchenpa, I will trace the psychological dimension of the thought and spiritual practice of Dzogchen, also known as Ati Yoga.

5

Between Classical Yoga and Dzogchen

Dzogchen

In this chapter I offer an overview on the differences between classic Indian yoga as represented by the *Yoga Sūtras* of Patañjali and of Ati Yoga, better known as Dzogchen, a stream of Tibetan Buddhism. The next chapter will focus on Dzogchen's psychological methods and the healing possibilities they hold for Dzogchen practitioners. Although the philosophy and method of classical Indian yoga are essentially contrary to those of Dzogchen, both are methods of yoga in its broadest sense: spiritual practice aimed at liberation, which is at the heart of Hinduism, Buddhism and Jainism. Before exploring the differences between classical Indian yoga and Dzogchen and how such differences can enrich and deepen our understanding of their psychological frameworks and therapeutic methods, I will provide a brief presentation of Dzogchen, which translates to "great perfection."

In term of its historical context, one of the main protagonists of Dzogchen, in its transmission from generation to generation, is Padmasambhava, who lived in the eighth century. When the Tibetan king Trisong Detsen founded the first Tibetan Buddhist temple and monastery, he invited Padmasambhava to perform shamanic rites related to water in the dry area of the first Buddhist monastery at Samyé. Thereafter, Padmasambhava taught the tantric practices of transformation known as the Vajrayāna and Dzogchen to an intimate audience. Padmasambhava then placed other teachings, known as the "treasures," in several sites in Tibet to be revealed by later generations. By that hermeneutic device, the origins of a tradition of "treasure revealers" would emerge in the eleventh century. This lay tantric practitioner became a well-known figure in Tibet, and was eventually hailed as the "second Buddha." He became the object of many devotional and ritualistic practices and has remained so throughout the history of Tibetan Buddhism.

One of the earliest texts on the early Dzogchen is *A Lamp for the Eye in Contemplation*, composed by ninth-century Tibetan scholar Nubchen Yeshe. The text is considered the most historically important treatise on Dzogchen, and it includes three other Buddhist philosophical views and practice. The text was discovered in 1900 in the Dunhuang Caves, which had been walled up in the eleventh century. The caves are close to the city of Dunhuang, China, situated on the Silk Road at a crossroads of cultural and religious importance. The earliest esoteric texts, tantras found in the caves, date from 790 to 851, when Dunhuang was under Tibetan rule.[1]

Dzogchen is about the discovery of one's intrinsic awareness as inseparable from one's natural mind, and it deals with the experience of this state. Natural awareness precedes specific content in the ordinary conditioned mind and precedes the thoughts that arise in it, which are the reflections of the psychological, cultural and social conditioning of the practitioner. Abiding in the nature of mind, stripped of content, allows one to extricate oneself from the cycle of suffering one is subjected to. However, humans do not recognize the nature of their mind. They do not recognize that their mind is originally clear and lucid, and therefore they undergo a split from a non-dual existence abiding in natural awareness to a dualistic existence between the subjective sense of being and the world of phenomena.

As much as Dzogchen and classical Indian yoga are both methods of yoga in its broadest sense—spiritual practice aimed at liberation—the philosophy and practice of classical Indian yoga is contrary to that of Dzogchen. These differences represent an interesting polarization between the two methods, reflecting the tension between intensive and gradual yoga practice and non-active, effortless Dzogchen. Such polarization raises philosophical questions in relation to the status of practice, its importance, and its application on the way to liberation, questions such as: Is gradual activity, whether physical or mental, likely to lead to a release from the cycle of action and consequences? Is it possible to realize the nature of mind without taking any action? Is the step-by-step practice of Patañjali's yoga necessary only because it trains and prepares one for liberation, or does it have the real, direct ability to bring the practitioner to liberation?

Patañjali's yoga is implemented within a continuous process of the cultivation of virtues and skills, such as uninvolved awareness (*vairāgya*), meditation and discernment between the two principles of realty: pure awareness or core true Selfhood, *puruṣa*, and the matter or the world of phenomena, *prakṛti*, constituting a dualistic philosophical framework. Patañjali's yoga is based on methods that enable gradual and continuous progress toward the realization of yoga. Such gradual approach is evident in the framework of yoga practice entailed in the eight limbs of yoga indicated in Patañjali's text: *yama* (abstinences) and *niyama* (observances). Both constitute the moral and ethical yogic rules. *Āsana* constitutes physical postures, *prāṇāyāma* is control of one's vital energy by means of breath exercises, *pratyāhāra* is withdrawal of the senses, *dhāraṇā* is an established attentive meditation, *dhyāna* is sustained and enduring meditation, and *samādhi* is intense meditative absorption or trance-like concentration. *Samādhi* itself is also practiced by stages as dependent on various objects: inner, external, subtle or gross, accompanied by or without a concept culminating in objectless meditative absorption.[2] Even though the practices of the eight limbs could also be practiced in parallel, not only one by one, their actual implementation is still gradual within as an active application progressing toward liberation.

The gradual path of classic Indian yoga rests on the obvious common presumption that it is desirable to change and cultivate ethical behavior and physical and mental health, and to practice meditation in order to realize liberation. It is based on the understanding that we are born and live in a state of ignorance of our true Self, hence the distorted, partial and relative knowledge we have of reality, which we seek to overcome or unveil. Yoga is involved with effort predicated on the belief that there is somewhere to be going to, such as achieving the next level on the yogic path. This includes either ethical, physical, mental or spiritual changes, improvements, or achievements as something that we hope to be gaining, which is different from the state we are currently in. The gradual path is based on the idea that practice should be implemented now in order to achieve good health, physical flexibility, stress release, peace, liberation, etc. in the future.

Dzogchen, on the other hand, is characterized by the immediate realization of Buddha nature: one's inherent natural awareness. Immediacy means the absence of any kind of mediation, study, activity, effort, accumulation of merits, religious beliefs in a supernatural entity, or philosophical concepts. It is the realization of Buddha nature through non-action, independent of any strategy of spiritual practice, gradual or intentional, and without even following the principle of non-action. Dzogchen rests on the assumption that our present state is one of perfection and liberation; it is our inherent natural state. In other words, it is already in our possession, and there is no need to take action or practice in order to achieve what is already our natural state. However, we do not recognize our natural liberated state, because human existence is filled with ignorance, misconception, partial and relative knowledge, and suffering, all of which constitutes our ordinary mind. Once one's ordinary mind and its mental constructs are deconstructed, shown to be empty of independent origin or absolute cause, the natural state of pure primordial awareness immediately dawns in one's mind as it realizes its natural awareness. Mental constructs are for example ideas, thoughts, meanings, perceptions, strategies and expectations that are also associated with spiritual practice, because they are all a product of mental activity, while pure primordial awareness cannot be a product of any action, including meditation.

The Dalai Lama asserts that Dzogchen is a unique path because it is based solely on the natural and inherent awareness shared by humans.[3] That is, meditative stability is an organic quality of natural awareness, just as heat is inherent to fire. Therefore, natural meditative stability is a means for continuously abiding in natural awareness, but it is also the goal. Therefore, natural awareness is both the means and the end.

Such a path is predicated on the notions of non-activity, effortlessness, and the here and now, because there is no action that can produce or generate liberation synonymous with the realization of one's true nature. Actions produce results, and one's true nature cannot be a result of any action, mental or physical, as it can never become an object. The moment one objectifies or labels their true nature, they separate themselves from that innate, pure awareness and return to their ordinary discursive mind, with its tendencies for objectification; that is, going after objects in the same way metal is attracted to magnet. When coming in contact with a sense object, the causes of affliction are stirred, clouding one's clarity and compelling one to act. Actions bring results that are the bed seed for future actions, which means that one is then locked in karmic cycles.

So non-action is synonymous with liberation from the compulsion to act. It is different from spontaneous or unpremeditated actions. Differentiating between acts of compulsion and acts of spontaneity reasonably explain the range of activities which were carried out by those enlightened ones who realized their intrinsic nature of mind, because non-action does not necessarily stand for a total absence of action. Liberated minds act spontaneously, responding (not reacting) appropriately to given circumstances. The modern notion of compulsive behavior is about being forced to act as a result of anxiety characterized by uncontrollable, unwanted thoughts and repetitive and ritualized behaviors. In the same manner, meditation and certain spiritual practices can become repetitive and ritualized behaviors when carried out by practitioners motivated by obsession, competitiveness, and the like. That is to say, one is then conditioned by negative or positive thoughts or by actions.

Going back in time, Nubchen Yeshe examines in *A Lamp for the Eye in Contemplation* how the immediate and non-gradual path of Dzogchen and its non-action component are understood in terms of a practice. According to Nubchen Yeshe, Dzogchen meditation includes two components: methods regarding how to discipline the body (*lus kyi bzhag thabs*) and methods regarding how to access the mind (*sems kyi 'jug thabs*). On the physical methods, Nubchen states:

> [In this system] there is no [specific] bodily discipline like [that of] the lower yogas of development, because it is free of any notion of bodily grasping or attachment. Thus, there are no definite methods regarding how to position the body. However, if one asks, "Does one reject [all the bodily discipline], such as cross-legged sitting and so forth, of the lower [vehicles]," [my response is that] one does not reject them

> as long as one does not grasp [or attach oneself] to the body. Nor does one accept them intentionally. [In that way] there is no contradiction in sitting cross legged, lying down facing up or down, or stretching in whatever way whatsoever. The practice of yoga itself makes anything into bliss, and laziness is [surely] a wrong action.[4]

Non-action in terms of not employing physical postures means that there are no physical postures as part of a plan or strategy that one might exercise as a means to enhance the state of meditation, or to access one's natural state. Physical postures cannot be a means to accessing one's natural state, because it is free of any premeditated strategy. Whatever the body posture is, that is the position of practice of stabilizing the natural state for the one who already abides in that state, as such physical postures are free from attachment to notions of loss and gain. Such physical postures not rooted in attachment should not be avoided, because avoidance here means laziness, which is a wrong action.

Patañjali mentions repeated activity (*abhyāsa*) and open, uninvolved awareness (*vairāgya*) as complementary forces in the physical dimension of yoga as well: "*Āsana* [yogic posture] is comfortably stable."[5] This means that the repeated active effort, *abhyāsa*, leads to maintaining a stable posture for long durations, and at the same time the practitioner is comfortable and relaxed in *vairāgya* (dispassion, or intended uninvolved awareness). There is no striving for achievement related to performing the posture or judgment about its quality; one should just abide in it. It seems Patañjali and Nubchen's approaches differ much more than being merely a matter of the themes they chose to emphasize. Patañjali prescribes an activity, a posture accompanied with the mental attitude of dispassion or uninvolved awareness. Such an attitude is dependent on the posture. Also, meditation is dependent on the posture and accompanied by intended uninvolved awareness. However, Nubchen stresses the notion of abiding in meditative absorption or natural awareness without intentionally adopting a posture or being attached to or rejecting one. Such abiding is independent of postures, ideas or beliefs.

As for methods of engaging the mind, Nubchen states that:

> It is an engaging without engagement. It is the suchness of reality that does not reify anything whatsoever and that naturally illuminates the essence of the great non-conceptual nature or being. Consequently the realization of non-engaging is known as engaging.[6]

What Nubchen is referring to here is the nature of mind, the awakened mind which cannot be accessed by any planned action, including a mental one. By "non-engaging," he means that if one can abide in a state which is unfabricated or uncontrived of natural meditative absorption, arrived at without any premeditated strategy, one will realize this engagement with the suchness of reality, a realization which is equal to the nature of mind. That is, one will see reality as it is. Therefore, if one makes any attempt to engage the nature of mind it would be fabricated, as it cannot be accessed by means of a physical or a mental activity. It is independent of any object. On the other hand, if one attempts to refrain from any engagement with any mental content, the very act of such avoidance is a strategy that may be a hindrance to engaging the nature of mind. Therefore, Nubchen points to relinquishment or abandonment of any strategic activity aimed to engage or access the nature of mind. Nubchen does not provide specific and committed instructions applicable to body and mind practices, but he indicates the notion of remaining unattached to a posture and independent of it, and abandoning meditative techniques intended to access the nature of the mind, allowing it to be carefree. In any case, methods of practice for the body and mind—physical and mental activities—are performed without any attachment to the methods themselves, their outcomes, and any loss or gain and pain or pleasure they might cause.

Non-action cannot refer to a total absence of action, but to activities that are not rooted in attachment, those that can fuel one's craving to what is pleasing, safe, certain and eternal. Otherwise, how can a range of activities, from eating, traveling, teaching, writing, debating and establishing monasteries be explained? How such activities carried out by those who realized essential mind, such as Nubchen Yeshe, Longchenpa and Padmasambhava, or even Tibetan Buddhist teacher and tantric master Gampopa Sonam Rinchen (1079–1153) and Tibetan Buddhist teacher and warrior Lama Zhang (1122–1193), be understood?

Philosophically speaking, Patañjali's philosophical system is based on two principles of realty: pure awareness or core true Selfhood (*puruṣa*), and the world of phenomena (*prakṛti*). The world of *prakṛti* includes both the external world and the inner phenomenal self, the individual; namely, the "I" in its existential and mundane sense. The principle of awareness is beyond body and mind; it is the "real" or "pure" Self (*puruṣa*). Suffering stems from the confusion between these two principles and from not recognizing them for what they are.[7] The confusing connection between the true Self and the world of phenomena can be pulled apart by means of discerning insight or wisdom that recognizes that they are fundamentally different and originally apart.[8] Such discerning wisdom is a key to liberation.

Dzogchen is extensively expressed and discussed in the works of Longchenpa, on which I intend to base my exploration of Dzogchen philosophy and psychology. Longchen Rabjampa (Longchenpa, or Klong chen rab 'byams pa, 1308–1364) was born in the fourteenth century to a poor family of the marginalized Nyingmapa (or rNying ma pa, the second-largest Buddhist sect in Tibet) and fled to the "demonic" land of Bhutan. He had turned away from monastic institutions and lived an austere life with his teacher in the open, exposed to the elements. He eventually returned to Tibet in 1360, after settling a dispute with Changchub Gyeltshen (Ta'i Si tu Byang chub rgyal mtshan), the ruler of Tibet at the time. He died in Tibet three years later.

Longchenpa was known for his tendency to sharply criticize the prevailing socio-religious-political structures and to oppose the dominant philosophical views and spiritual praxis. In spite of his humble background, Longchenpa became one of the greatest teachers and scholars of the Dzogchen tradition. Seven hundred years after his death, his work is still studied by many Tibetan Buddhists, mainly the Nyingmapas sect and Western Buddhist followers and scholars interested in the Great Perfection, as well as the fourteenth Dalai Lama. Longchenpa is considered both a legend and a luminary, and his encyclopedic poetic and philosophical works are still held in high esteem. He left behind him some 307 works, mainly writings of philosophy, poetry and prose. Although at times it is difficult to date his works, he left behind an organized catalog that has helped historians trace the chronological sequence of his writings and to follow the development of his thought.[9] The works of Longchenpa provide a profound psychological framework for understanding the human psyche.

My intention in reading Longchenpa's works is to extend their boundaries beyond the existing historical, philosophical or philological commentaries, exploring further "unconsidered" meanings within the theme of the theory and practice of the psychology of yoga. This seems an urgent task when reviewing the limited academic research dedicated to Longchenpa, as most work has been carried out from the viewpoints of historical criticism, phenomenology, doxography, literary studies of rhetoric and philology, but not his own theory and practice of the psychology of yoga. In studying the life and teachings of Longchenpa, it becomes evident that among academic circles of the West his doctrine has not generated much interest, thus the academic research dedicated to him so far has been limited. This is surprising, considering the significance of his contributions to Tibetan Buddhism and the way he is perceived by the Tibetan tradition and its scholars. It can probably be firstly explained by the sheer difficulty of translating his writings, and secondly by the possibility that other figures, such as Nāgārjuna, Candrakīrti, Vasubandhu and Śaṅkara, seem more interesting for philosophers and researchers, offering more raw material for research in many areas of Buddhism: language, logic, epistemology, ontology and comparative studies.[10]

However, as Herbert Guenther, one of the most original and highly regarded pioneers in the research of Dzogchen puts it:

> Longchen Rabjampa (Klong-chen rab-'byams-pa) is hailed as a second Buddha and certainly the greatest thinker in the Old Tradition (rnying-ma-pa) ... Longchen Rabjampa is concerned with the exploration of lived-through experience, not with an intellectual parlour game of quantifications of fetish-words that have no longer any meaning because they have become divorced from experience.[11]

That is to say, Longchenpa is hailed as a second Buddha, and such a title is not imparted lightly, but it tells us about the high status Longchenpa achieved in Tibet. He is perceived by Guenther to be a thinker-philosopher interested not in forming mere theories, but in pointing to the "way to be" in the world and integrating it with a life of realization. Longchenpa's philosophy contains a significant pragmatic or existential aspect, which will be taken into consideration when examining his theory and practice of the psychology of his Ati Yoga.

Longchenpa's Dzogchen is about non-duality, in which one's nature of mind is integrated with the world of phenomena, seeing it as it is and recognizing its fundamental base: primordial natural awareness endowed with potentiality. Our ordinary mind is in *samsara* and is subjected to karma—thoughts, feelings, and endless events arising from a samsaric existence.

Samsara and *nirvana* are two primary dimensions that exist simultaneously and seem to express an orderly and coherent view. But in this view, there is also a difficulty: On the one hand, the basis on which the world of phenomena is woven is primordially pure (*nirvana*), and on the other hand it is also associated with ignorance, occupied with mental and physical patterns and latent habitual tendencies (*samsara*). If so, such a base cannot be pure. It loses its non-dual status. In other words, in order for the status of non-duality to be valid, both dimensions, *samsara* and *nirvana*, must be identical.

However, Longchenpa believes that an identity between the pure primary basis and the phenomenal basis does not necessarily have to exist.[12] He explains the differences between them by means of a metaphor. The pure primary basis, which bears the potential to manifest, is like clear water, free of mud, while the basis of the world of phenomena is like murky water. The murky water distorts the natural and clear awareness and its inherent wisdom and prevents it from concrete manifestation. The metaphor suggests that the concealed habitual tendencies and the samsaric mental and physical imprints are not intrinsic to the *dharmakāya*, or pure primary basis. One may discern between two different aspects of water: murky and clear. However, the Tibetolog David Higgins argues that while the two aspects cannot be separated, there is a relationship of precedence, such as between founder and the founded. The primary and pure base of awareness precedes the world of phenomena, which arises from the base, uninterrupted, as an expression of its concealed potentiality.[13]

Now that we have established an overview entailing the differences between yoga as a gradual path in terms of spiritual practice and based on a dualistic philosophy, and Dzogchen as an immediate spiritual path that is about non-dualism, what would be the self-perceptions, presumptions or beliefs embedded in each one them? As a broad statement, the gradual path of classical yoga is predicated on the need for change, for improvement or repair toward liberation. Such need stems from the perception or belief that what is happening to one is not satisfactory and that there is a need for them to be somewhere else doing something else, or to be other than the way one is if one wanted to be fulfilled, realized or content. Such need for change, for improvement, or for repair is covertly embedded within the practices on the gradual path, as these practices are propelled by the belief that there is something else to get in the future.

The gradual path is a process within the psychology of yoga. The more one practices the cultivation of the opposite—which requires an ongoing reflection and analysis of the consequences of one's negative conduct—and the more one uses yoga practice to cultivate mental imprints that induce peace and silence (*saṃskāras* of the *nirodha* type), the more such mental imprints will dominate and outdo the ones that bear pain and suffering (*saṃskāras* of the *vyutthāna* type). Only when the mental imprints that bear pain and suffering are dissolved, obstructed or silenced will the mind become imperturbable, allowing the practitioner to experience an increasing sense of relief. A practitioner of yoga who persistently and systematically fosters the *nirodha* type of *saṃskāras* achieves not only the release of the mind from the grip of the *vyutthāna* type, but also the rise of the discerning insight and total concentration, and with it the dawn of Self-knowledge. Such a yogic project definitely implies a vigilant process implemented over time.

A path of immediacy such as Dzogchen offers an alternative predicated on the notion that one's true nature is already perfect the way it is, and that there is nothing more one needs. One is already enlightened, which is one's intrinsic natural state of being; however, one does not realize it yet. The path of immediacy is covertly embedded within the notion that whatever is happening is the manifestation of the natural mind and it can't be something else. Hence, there is nothing to get, since one is already realized. The ideas that one's experience can displace another and that there is more to this experience are simply mental constructs, products of imagination. When such mental constructs arise and manifest in terms of beliefs that are acted out in a pattern of behaviors, and when emotional reactions are deconstructed, pure awareness immediately permeates one's mind as Self-realization. The deconstruction can occur by means of analytical mediation, or by honestly recognizing one's emotions at work, owning them and relaxing within them, neither grasping nor pushing them away, or with a certain Dzogchen practice of *Rushen*, which is similar to a cathartic process. Without this constant reflection, it is nearly impossible to lessen the causes of affliction.

The polarity discussed above between the principle of gradualism in yoga practice and the principle of immediacy is also expressed in the psychological methods of yoga and Dzogchen, along with the therapeutic possibilities they offer. At the same time, it is important to mention and emphasize that both classic Indian yoga and Dzogchen share a similar psychological framework that has been discussed in the introduction and first chapter. It entails the notions of suffering, ignorance (Skt. *avidyā*, Tib. *marigpa*), subliminal mental imprints (Skt. *saṃskāras*, Tib. *du-je*), patterns of behavior (Skt. *Vāsanās*, Tib. *bag-chags*), and causes of addiction (Skt. *kleśas*, Tib. *nyon mongs*). The differences between the gradual yogic path and the Dzogchen path of immediacy translate in the psychological methods.

Given that in Chapter 2 and 3 I discussed Patañjali's psychological method of cultivation of opposites, in the next chapter I shall show the psychological methods of Dzogchen that relate to the release of the emotional and mental burden that the practitioner has accumulated without being aware of it, and to the release of oppressive thoughts. Practicing these methods shakes the practitioner out of his habits, leading to a state of effortless contemplation that enables him to realize his innate natural mind.

How do these methods actually help the yoga practitioner loosen the grip of his habitual tendencies? For that, we will turn in the next chapter to the writings of the fourteenth-century Tibetan scholar and teacher Longchenpa to focus on the psychological dimension of Dzogchen as expressed in his thought and practice.

6

The Psychology of Tibetan Dzogchen
Ati Yoga

The polarity discussed in the previous chapter between the principle of gradualism in yoga practice and the principle of immediacy is also expressed in the psychological methods of yoga and Dzogchen, along with the therapeutic possibilities they offer. At the same time, it is important to mention and emphasize that both classic Indian yoga and Dzogchen share a similar psychological framework that has been discussed in the introduction and first chapter.

The psychological dimension of Dzogchen, as expressed in Longchenpa's thought and practice, centers on the Tibetan term *bag chags* (which is similar to the term *vāsanā* in Sanskrit), meaning "a pattern of behavior" or "habitual tendency." As in the psychological theory of the Indian *sūtras*, for Longchenpa the term also represents hidden mental imprints whose effect on the personality is prolonged.[1] In other words, with the use of this term, Longchenpa also points to the organization of mental imprints into configured units that turn into patterns of behavior and character.[2] This term concerns all the mental imprints that are stored at the base of the mind, and they have the potential to manifest into the entire range of human experiences.

The base of mind has three aspects: somatic, psychological and epistemological. The somatic aspect—the body distinct from the mind—relates to the formations of endless mental imprints which are responsible for the manifestation of the body in all its systems.[3] According to this aspect, the processes are not only physical, but also metaphysiological; that is, processes that take place in the centers (cakras) and the metapsychic channels.[4] The view is that the body consists of a collection of physical and subtle metaphysical channels or neural channels, and their control is achieved through yoga postures, breathing exercises, guided imagery and meditation.[5] The psychological aspect includes the conscious and the unconscious realms of the human psyche. This aspect addresses the situation in which the individual does not identify innate natural awareness and does not recognize it. Thus, the mental imprints, tendencies, habits and patterns of behavior perpetuate the individual's involvement in conditioned existence.[6] In such a state, the mental imprints mature into a set of beliefs, attitudes, emotions and actions, all of which may create new patterns of mental imprints. These have the potential to manifest and become concrete. They may appear under certain circumstances which provoke them and instigate one to act. Alternatively, one can recognize his innate, pure, natural awareness, which originally is not involved with the psychological and mental processes. Abiding in one's innate, pure, natural awareness, one is free from the discourse about the world of phenomena and the distractions it presents. Such a recognition of one's innate, pure, natural awareness enables one to dismantle thoughts, emotions, actions and behaviors dictated by mental imprints and to release them.

The ordinary human mind is not pure mental space. Data such as colors, flavors and odors are absorbed through sensory contact with external objects and processed in the mind, interpreted and deciphered by categories of thought that are nothing but remnants of previous experiences. This function defines the inner subjective feeling of the person, and it is sufficient to name and interpret such a feeling for it to become an object. Thus, even a subjective feeling becomes in our thought processes an object to which we attribute concrete reality. The result is the perpetuation of the duality between persons and the world of objects. Duality causes the perpetuation of mental or physical activity with respect to a particular object: "I love it" or "I dislike it," "I want it" or "I don't want it," and so on.

One therefore believes that the world of phenomena is a separate world, so that one is preoccupied with the relationship between oneself and the world of objects and events. This dichotomy represents the dualism of a dual existence. In fact, the mind is a set of mental, emotional, and behavioral variables. It is occupied with a misconception about the separation between subjective consciousness and the world of phenomena, and this separation is realized both through unconscious cognitive processes and the involvement with the world of phenomena.

Data received through sensory contact with external objects are processed, deciphered and interpreted according to thought categories. These mental processes are associated with labeling, evaluation and judgment, and as such they distort the perception of the object. The object then is seen not as it is, but through subjective mental processes. That is to say, as the duality of the "I" and the "other" is formed, we will be forced to accept and enjoy certain situations while rejecting or tolerating others. For example, if the feeling of an event or object was pleasant or painful, then the event or object itself would be sorted and marked as tempting or threatening, accordingly. Such labeling may trigger an automatic emotional response, such as longing, desire, fear, anger or aggression. These emotional responses can move the individual into action that will create and accumulate further karma.

Another aspect of mind is the epistemological one. It concerns the samsaric dimension of existence, the absence of recognition of natural awareness (which exists from the very beginning). In other words, the ignorance of natural awareness is fertile ground for the existence of *samsara*. It refers to an existence within a cycle of birth and death as a karmic cycle of incarnations, a purposeless existence. One who has not yet become aware of the innate awareness inherent in one strays into phenomenal existence. Liberation from such existence is at the basis of the spiritual search. Longchenpa compares this aspect of the *samsara* to the state of mind that continually dwells in the wrong perception.[7] Such a misconception is rooted in an internal system of mental imprints, beliefs, views, and ideas that have been imprinted in the mind. The budding of such a system exists within us from birth and continues to develop over time, according to the circumstances and events that characterize human existence, and it perpetuates the experience of pain. It represents an opposite situation to that of recognizing and realizing natural awareness. This misconception causes human beings to be subjected to a conditioned existence, one driven by mental imprints, despite their potential to identify the natural, clear awareness emptied of all content.

The psychological aspect of the world of phenomena and of human experience is expressed in layers of hidden habitual tendencies that lie in the depths of our memory and are composed of emotions and thoughts. They have the raw potential to activate the mind and generate experiences and events, which will also be the seeds of future repeated patterns and behaviors. What then are the psychological methods that Longchenpa proposes to use to extricate us from this cyclical karma?

Emotions are hardly mentioned in Dzogchen texts, and it is possible that they were chiefly addressed in the oral tradition. It is also possible that emotions are not part of the Dzogchen view of natural awareness, which in fact transcends emotions, both positive and negative. The original, pristine Dzogchen practice is based on a stable meditative absorption that occurs naturally. Its very practice indicates that the practitioner already has an experience of natural awareness. He is able to abide in natural awareness without resorting to other means or meditation of any other kind, while at the same merging and integrating with the world of phenomena. Such a steadfast meditative absorption is an intrinsically organic quality of natural awareness, just as wetness is inherent to water. This makes the stable meditative absorption a means for continuously abiding in natural awareness, but it is also the goal. Natural awareness is both the means and the end in that they are identical, a non-duality.

Philosophically speaking, Dzogchen binds and unifies the means with the end, thus avoiding the problematic duality or dichotomy of subject and object, cause and effect, means and purpose. Only through the practice of the natural meditation of Dzogchen by a steady and sustained rest in natural awareness one can justifiably claim that Dzogchen is non-dual.

Psychological Methods in Dzogchen

While a practitioner of Dzogchen is in the process of awakening to the state of natural awareness, he remains exposed to challenging circumstances, even if he is acquainted with the state and has been abiding in it for certain periods of time. Circumstances are responsible for triggering mental imprints and generating certain thoughts and feelings for the practitioner that may capture him in their own thicket. They may drive him to act, distort his perception of reality as to the circumstances, and this may cause pain and suffering for the practitioner and others.

The practitioner of Dzogchen continues to be exposed to challenging possibilities and circumstances, mainly because of the latent nature of mental imprints and habitual tendencies, which makes it difficult for him to identify, undo and control them. The mental imprints are subconscious, and so hidden from consciousness that it is almost impossible to expose them. They can only be exposed if one constantly looks at their symptoms. Then perhaps it will be possible to identify them, diagnose them, and treat them accordingly. As long as the subjugating power of these imprints is not undone, their inherent potential may be activated and actualized in appropriate circumstances, and it may drive the person into conditional behavior. They are like a seed, which under the right conditions sprouts and grows into a tree that will yield fruit, and so forth. It seems that Longchenpa is aware of these difficulties, and offers the following practice:

> Visit places that generate blessed, frightening or painful births, at the top of a mountain, in a cemetery, or in an abandoned valley. With the body you jump, run, dance and make gestures, with Speech you shout, sing, lament and cry, with the mind you imagine the states of happiness and suffering of the six modes of being, and then in one moment, diligently and determinedly, practice self-liberation ... Then you will soon achieve the highest and most common achievements, and all the negative circumstances, the lack of harmony, all the obstacles without exception, will dissipate.[8]

Although the purpose of the practice is to lead to the discernment between the phenomenal ordinary mind and the naked, clear, natural mind, I will analyze the practice from a psychological perspective in an attempt to extract from it the components that can undo patterns of behavior resulting from mental imprints.

Longchenpa is aware that the mental imprints are latent and concealed, and he therefore proposes to the Dzogchen practitioner to visit places where there is certain atmosphere: a mountain with a magnificent primal landscape or a burial ground that can evoke a wide range of thoughts, emotions and sensations. This instruction is meant to stimulate a variety of impressions and feelings, ranging from pain and suffering to happiness and blessed existence. The practitioner is guided to give full and uncontrolled expression to the sensations, sounds, emotions and thoughts that arise in his body, voice and mind in reaction to the atmosphere of the place. An uncontrolled expression can be anything that comes to mind and releases all restraint, so that the emotions are relieved of their burden to the point of exhaustion. The practitioner is then instructed to sit and observe the emotions and thoughts that arise without trying to suppress or block them; he is only required to recognize and acknowledge them. He observes them without being captivated by them. Then they are released, by themselves, in the same way that a snake uncoils itself; this is "self-liberation." The practice, therefore, is not only somatic and cognitive but also contemplative.

The somatic component of this practice relates to motor functions which release an emotional burden, such as the sounding of different sounds, of crying, laughter, wailing or gibberish. There may also be movements, such as chaotic dance, crawling, jumping, intensive end-to-end walking, imitative movements of imaginary animals, and all that arise in an uncensored mind. These actions lead to a release of the accumulated emotional and mental burden, and discharge thoughts and emotions that were imprisoned without one's awareness. They shake up the practitioner, moving him away from his patterns of reactions and expressions.

The cognitive component of the practice relates to the visualization of the six modes of existence, a long and weary process. The six modes of existence are the dimension of the gods, the semi-gods, animals, human beings, hungry spirits, and the dimension of inferno. Buddhism believes that one's mind may reincarnate in one of those modes in accordance with the karma that one has accumulated. Each of the six modes of existence represents emotions that bind those who experience them to *samsara*, to the cycle of suffering, of birth and death. The dimension of gods is characterized by pride and superiority. The dimension of the semi-gods is characterized by jealousy of the gods. They also experience pain due to the death of their comrades in battles with the gods. The animal dimension of existence is characterized by fear, the constant need for survival, and the need to hunt. The dimension of human existence is characterized by desire in all its forms: for sex, money, knowledge, understanding and recognition. The dimension of the hungry ghosts is characterized by thirst, starvation, and the desire for external objects that will satisfy their compulsive attachments. The dimension of inferno is characterized by anger and aggression. The emotions and feelings that characterize every dimension of existence are visible, and they manifest in daily situations that every living creature experiences, regardless of the belief in the Buddhist cosmology of the cycle of birth and death.

In this practice, the practitioner is guided to imagine freely, in a vivid unplanned visualization, and to wonder what he would have had if he had been incarnated into one of these dimensions of existence, and what the taste of life might have been. The vital visualization of the six dimensions of existence and the enjoyment of pleasure, sorrow, and understanding of the suffering involved in these dimensions enable the practitioner to undo his habitual tendencies toward attachments and aversion. The gain, loss, pleasure and pain associated with these habitual tendencies are driven by deep dissatisfaction, as are the emotions and feelings that characterize the six dimensions of existence. Reflecting on the nature of attachment during the process of visualization may bring about the insight that everything is the result of mental imprints and processes that are without cause being empty of independent origin. Such an insight may open a door to one's intrinsic nature of mind and natural awareness, which is naked of perceptions, attachments, tendencies and passions, and of any mental content.

After the practitioner acts out of the emotions that have arisen under the influence of the environment he has experienced,[9] and after expressing them to the point of exhaustion, his compulsive thoughts and feelings may be spontaneously released. That is, at this stage of the practice, the practitioner does not seek to pursue and process these feelings and thoughts, nor to reject them, suppress them, or act under their influence. His awareness is free. It is no longer dependent on obsessive or deliberate emotions. Also, thoughts and emotions are dismantled and dissolved by themselves in the absence of the attention that fuels them. The self-release from reactive emotions takes place within the practitioner through a process of being aware of and abiding in his innate natural mind. This is the purpose of the practice.

According to Longchenpa, the somatic and cognitive components of the practice contain structured and unstructured processes that release tension and anxiety through expressing hidden, imprisoned thoughts and emotions. This intense release leads to exhaustion, which plays a central role in the occurrence of self-liberation. It is exhaustion that makes it possible to stop all mental activity and sink into a state of indifferent openness,[10] by giving up the tension associated with the tense alertness of defense mechanisms. This is a condition that may ultimately lead to the dawn of self-liberated natural awareness.

The process that Longchenpa suggests somewhat resembles catharsis, a process that frees stress and anxiety by expressing feelings that are imprisoned, unconscious, restrained or suppressed. In cathartic processes, thoughts and emotions arise and flood the mind and body, defusing their energy. Although there are cultural and historical differences between Greek Aristotelian philosophy and the Tibetan Dzogchen of Longchenpa, they seem to share the concept of catharsis and its efficacy in releasing the emotional and mental burden accumulated in one's psyche, though a deeper comparative study would be necessary to fully explore their respective uses of this concept.

Even if for certain periods of time the mature Dzogchen practitioner manages to remain in a state of natural awareness, there will almost always be periods of time that he will not abide in such a state. Then he will be exposed to the triggering of mental imprints, thoughts and feelings that may trap him in their own tangle. Moreover, with the release of emotions under the influence of the physical, somatic and cognitive cathartic processes, the mental defenses usually return to their previous intensity;[11] depending, of course, on how solid, powerful, and established the practitioner's defense mechanisms are.

In modern psychology, catharsis is a method based on the view that emotional problems can be addressed effectively if patients express repressed emotions, such as grief and anger. However, catharsis is not a method in itself. Psychologist Barry Guinagh (1941–2019) has argued that the concept of catharsis has been integrated into modern psychological approaches, especially in cognitive psychology, an approach that seeks to create a mental change by working through the patient's ways of thinking. The underlying assumption is that emotional problems are best solved when the patient changes his patterns of thinking and behaving, as well as his values and beliefs when they do not match his day-to-day reality. In addition, according to the cognitive approach, the patient is encouraged to modify his emotional response to his environment.[12]

In Dzogchen practice, the more the practitioner practices the exhausting, cathartic practice, and the longer he may abide in the natural state, the less he is affected by the triggering of the mental imprints. Longchenpa's method lacks the central principle of modern psychology: the conscious attempt to recall experiences in order to alter their effect on us, especially the formative experiences that have shaped our fundamental self-perception.

Longchenpa's goal also differs from that of modern psychology. He seeks to guide practitioners from the moment they discern between the phenomenal, ordinary mind and the natural, lucid mind to the moments of intimate familiarity with their intrinsic nature of mind. At this point emotions and tensions are released naturally, and practitioners contemplate and abide in natural awareness. Here is Longchenpa's instruction as to how to release emotions and tensions and to continue to contemplate and abide in natural awareness:

> When something unwanted falls into your lap, you have a negative reaction, such as anger, dislike, envy, upset, irritation, anxiety, depression, mental anguish, or fear of death and rebirth. When such reactions arise as a display due to dynamic energy, identify them as such. Do not renounce them, indulge in them, refine them away, transform them, look at them, or meditate on them. Rather, rest spontaneously in the single, naturally settled state of evenness, free of the proliferation and resolution of conceptual frameworks. Mind as a pure expanse of space, in which things vanish naturally and leave no trace, arises with intensity from within, pristinely lucid.[13]

In other words, when a person feels negative emotions such as anger, disgust, jealousy, depression and anxiety, he should not attempt to suppress, refine, ignore, alter, meditate on or clarify their essence. All that is required of him is to rest steadfastly in pure natural awareness without any conceptualization or labeling of the emotions.

Negative emotions provide raw material for training to recognize natural awareness. When these feelings appear, one must recognize them first by means of an open and non-conceptualizing mind. Then, as this skill is perfected, the negative emotions will release themselves, effortlessly and without notice. In other words, staying in this awareness allows the negative emotions that arise in the practitioner to dissipate without leaving any karmic trace. Their power will be lost, and they will no longer condition the practitioner to certain thoughts, activities or behaviors. They are like waves that rise from the sea and return to the sea without a trace. In this way, the practitioner can practice resting in natural awareness for long periods of time.

It is interesting to note that the method of natural release also relates to positive emotions, though it is not surprising, since often positive emotions are also associated with habitual tendencies and patterns of behavior. A natural release may occur when joy, associated with objects of desire and pleasure, is experienced in a state of rest and abiding in the natural awareness. In fact, identifying the natural state and non-verbally recognizing it (even without conceptualizing or labeling it) does not fuel such positive experiences and the actions that they may cause. Attachment to pleasurable experiences recorded in one's memory may drive one to replicate them time and again. However, in the natural state the objects of desire are experienced as they are.[14]

It is even surprising that the natural release method is also suitable for neutral feelings.[15] They appear when one makes sensory contact with an object toward which one is indifferent; it could equally be pleasant or unpleasant. The practitioner is guided not to direct his thoughts to the experience. He is required to identify the naked, natural awareness underlying the experience of the neutral feeling. He experiences the neutral sensory contact, and in this state feelings are released by themselves, in a manner likened to the long snake who uncoils itself from a complicated and difficult tangle.

Emotions should not be erased, but if one holds on to them, they can turn into rigid patterns of behavior. The practitioner should remain in open, natural awareness in the presence of desires, and at the same time allow self-liberation to occur naturally. "Let anger fade, fade away and disappear" is the advice known to every meditation practitioner. This advice means that the disciple must pay attention to the impulses and recognize them non-verbally without conceptualizing or labeling. He must adopt uninvolved awareness; that is, he must reflect on and consider feelings without following their automatic patterns of action. At first, applying these principles requires effort to focus one's attention, similar to Patañjali's method of *vairāgya* as uninvolved awareness. But over time, Longchenpa's natural self-liberation does not require great effort. This uninvolved awareness is similar to that of the higher order in Patañjali, the *para-vairāgya*, as a release from attachment or clinging.[16]

The Lines of Time and Place

It seems that until a practitioner of Dzogchen is skilled enough in continually abiding in natural awareness, he will be exposed to challenging situations where his feelings and emotions may be triggered time and again and blind him. For example, when one is angry, he is possessed and consumed by the object or the circumstance the anger is directed to, mostly to the degree of being irrational and blind to different understandings of the situation and to the consequences of such behavior for himself and the others subjected to his anger. Such situations clearly indicate that the repositories of mental imprints, tendencies and patterns of behavior have not yet been dismantled and fully emptied of their dynamic charge. If so, how can a practitioner generate and communicate compassion as a true expression of natural awareness, while his habitual tendencies stem from a whole set of internal psychological dynamics of which he is not aware?

After forty years of practicing the meditation methods of *madhyamaka* and the contemplative methods of Dzogchen, former Buddhist monk, scholar and teacher Peter Fenner argues that it takes a long time to develop the skill of natural release, or self-release.[17] American physician Elliott Dacher also believes that it takes a long time to develop mental tools such as awareness and attentiveness that help the practitioner recall the object he was concentrating on for his meditation, or careful observation that allows him to perceive situations in which his mind is distracted and wandering. In order for the wandering, distracted mind to return to rest within itself, the practitioner of meditation uses both of these tools while being aware of his breathing. He must persist, regardless of the number of times he is distracted, and regardless of the number of times he is required to return to abide in mindfulness and to let go of his tendency to be distracted and wander. And he must continue, regardless of the number of times he has been able to avoid following thoughts into the past, projecting them into the future or dealing with them in the present.[18] And what should the Dzogchen practitioner do until then? Will he continue to inflict pain and suffering on himself and others?

Here are two testimonies of Tibetan lamas (the concept of lama in Tibetan Buddhism is similar to the Indian guru) cited by Jack Kornfield.[19] They demonstrate that achieving higher states of awareness and remaining in them for a certain period of time does not guarantee the release of hidden mental and physical imprints, nor does it guarantee the dismantling of their potential or the change of patterns of behavior that are related to the causes of affliction in the short term. One lama tells the following story:

> When I came back, it was as if the twelve years of experiences in India and Tibet were a dream. The memory and value of those transcendental experiences was in some way a dream challenged by the culture shock of returning to my family and to work in the West. Old patterns came back surprisingly quickly. I got irritable, confused. I was not taking care of my body, I worried about money, about relationship. At the worst point, I feared that I was losing what I had learned. Then I realized that I could not live in some enlightened memory. What became clear is that spiritual practice is only what you are doing now. Anything else is a fantasy.[20]

In other words, it is not enough to devote oneself fully to the practice of Buddhism in India and Tibet for twelve years to break down old patterns of behavior. The return to Western culture awakened the mental imprints from their slumber, allowing them to regain their influence over the lama.

Another Tibetan Buddhist lama lost the connection to the physical and instinctive intelligence of the body, which he attributed to living in a world in which we are required to shield and ignore the pain:

> I saw a lot of pathological detachment from myself and others. In many years of working in renunciation or isolation, I have become attached to many things, but I have been careful to observe the ancient Buddhist customs that repress things and ignore them. I do not know how many *vipassanā* meditation teachers and how many lamas who lived with medical problems I met. One might say that disease is a natural part of the Buddha's first, noble truth about suffering. But most teachers neglected their bodies for many years. And what about me? I used to be proud of how relaxed and detached I could be, a man who never loses his temper or anger, lives beyond all pressures, maintains a steady mind. But what about my body? What into which organs have I repressed all these things, so that my health has been damaged? Today, twenty-five years later, I begin to respect my body, the need for rest, exercise, to find the physical intelligence I have lost so long ago.[21]

Although he developed a sophisticated ability to maintain a stable mind, emotional repression had a negative effect on his physical health. He ignored what his body was telling him, causing illness and physical distress.

John Welwood cites another example. One of his patients traveled to India at the age of seventeen to get away from her rich family, whom she felt did not love or understand her. She spent seven years in India and Nepal, studying and practicing with Tibetan teachers. She would withdraw for long periods of time to practice meditation, in which she reached powerful insights and experienced extended periods of happiness and inner freedom. Upon her return to Europe, she found it difficult to function. Nothing seemed to make sense. She married a charismatic man, and before she realized what was happening they had two children. Looking back, she said:

> This man was my shadow. He represented all the parts of myself I had run away from. I found him totally fascinating and became swept up in a course of events over which I had no control. Clearly, all my spiritual practice had not touched the rest of me—all the old fears, confusions, and unconscious patterns that hit me in the face when I returned to the West.[22]

Here too we see the gap between the protracted higher states of consciousness experienced by the practitioner and the concrete impact of latent mental impressions. As noted in the previous chapter, higher states of consciousness do not necessarily alleviate one's suffering in the phenomenal world. It appears that the patient's focus should have been on the emotional world of intimate relationships. The practice of meditation may serve as a spiritual bypass or an evasion of real and direct confrontation with emotions, relationships, and the demands of phenomenal existence. In such cases, meditation may be complemented by Western psychological methods, such as Miller's adaptation of the technique of EMDR discussed in chapter 4.

The Integration of an Awareness Devoid of Preferences with Modern Psychology

If until now yoga and modern psychology have been presented as distinct but complementary approaches, I will now examine the ways in which notions of natural awareness may be merged as a single, integrated method. How can the state of mind of non-duality, similar to that of Dzogchen, be integrated with modern psychology, and how can it help patients, as well as practitioners of Dzogchen?

Gary Nixon, a clinical psychologist who deals with addiction, has developed a therapeutic approach that integrates what he calls the "perspective of awareness devoid of any choice or preference." His approach is based on adopting a nonjudgmental attitude toward one's psychological problems in order to defuse difficult memories. His concept of "choiceless awareness" draws on Krishnamurti's statement that he is not afraid of the future, for in a state of non-judgmental total attentiveness, he has no fear.[23]

As described by American human rights activist and author John Prendergast (1963–),[24] Nixon asserts that he is able to remain in the presence of the choiceless awareness that reflects a given state of affairs in a non-judgmental, totally attentive manner as unpremeditated, unconditioned, effortless, responsive and complete awareness. He claims that he can navigate himself to such an awareness, present it and integrate it into the therapy session. During a dialogue in such a session, the patient discovers a deep sense of emptiness or absence, and learns from the therapist to rest and remain in a choiceless awareness while abandoning the personal stories that make up his identity.[25] Nixon reiterates that the key to his therapeutic work is acceptance and non-judgment, and they are applied according to the patient's capacity, as long as he is not affected by extreme mental, emotional and physical problems. He guides the patient to reach a state of mind of presence without preferences, and when both patient and therapist are in this state of awareness together, they process the psychological problem through dialogue. Then the patient is guided into a deeper state to reexperience the emotions associated with the psychological problem. Through this process the intensity of the experience subsides and dissipates.[26]

Nixon illustrates this process with the story of Myrna. At age seven, Myrna witnessed the sexual abuse of her friend by her friend's father. The traumatic memory of seeing blood pouring into the bathroom drain was etched in her mind. As she recalled this trauma in therapy, she began to hyperventilate and asked to stop the session. Nixon urged her not to leave the room but to try to observe what she was going through without judgment. She gathered up the courage to recall the mental picture of the traumatic event, and she began to tremble. Then Nixon asked her not to take a judgmental stance in light of the details of this mental picture. After a few minutes, it seemed that the tremor and the emotional intensity were beginning to fade, and she sat up suddenly, calm and still.

Myrna reported that the sense of calm she had felt continued to accompany her for several days, and she believed that a new process of healing had begun. Nixon points out that, before she met him, she had worked on the trauma intensely with other therapists and she brought this previous work into his therapeutic setting.[27] The turning point in the therapy session came about when Myrna was ready to reexperience the traumatic event in all its details. But would it be reasonable to assert that Myrna's newfound courage was a result of the encouragement she felt from the therapist's presence? Could it be that his suggestion to stay in choiceless awareness allowed her to examine the traumatic mental images stored in her memory? Other variables, such as the previous psychological work she had undergone to process the trauma, may have also contributed to Myrna's therapy under Nixon's guidance.

In Myrna's therapy with Nixon, there was no direct processing of latent mental imprints related to her attitudes toward men, sex, shame or secrecy. After several months of meetings with Nixon, Myrna returned to her former therapist. Myrna's fears seem to have subsided, thanks to her courage to look at the mental images of the traumatic event while remaining calm, despite the intense physical reaction she had experienced.

The therapeutic achievement, enabled by the cultivation of courage, can be described as the partial decomposition of mental imprints, such as "I am in danger," that were engraved in her mind during the traumatic event. It is reasonable to assume that other mental imprints remained unprocessed due to the short treatment period. According to Nixon and Prendergast, therapists who are able to rest and remain in the presence of choiceless awareness, abiding in non-duality, reflect to their patients their true nature: an awareness that precedes thoughts, feelings and sensations. Nixon and Prendergast assert that therapists differ in their degree of maturity and insight regarding their identity or natural awareness.[28]

This raises a number of questions, such as who is a qualified as a therapist of non-duality, and what is his level of ability to stay in awareness, without any of the preferences which precede the mind's discursive activity. Is there a clear standard regarding the ability of therapists to abide in choiceless awareness, and to recognize such awareness in others? One would need to understand why famous and brilliant teachers from various traditions of non-duality have suffered from serious behavioral problems that could not be resolved through the wisdom of non-duality. This question underscores that achieving higher states of awareness and abiding in such states for extended periods of time does not guarantee the release of hidden mental and physical imprints.

To what extent can psychological approaches that integrate methods of non-duality effectively treat compulsive behavior, psychosis, addictions, anxiety and depression? How do these approaches compare to therapeutic humanistic, behavioral, cognitive or drug approaches? Little empirical research has been done to address these questions. Longchenpa cautions against seeking the seductive magic solution of non-duality for problems such as anxiety or depression:

> When ... you have a negative reaction, such as anger, dislike, envy, upset, irritation, anxiety, depression, mental anguish, or fear of death and rebirth. When such reactions arise as a display due to dynamic energy, identify them as such. Do not renounce them, indulge in them, refine them away, transform them, look at them, or meditate on them. Rather, rest spontaneously in the single, naturally settled state of evenness, free of the proliferation and resolution of conceptual frameworks.[29]

A person who seeks help may believe that he will only be liberated from the causes of affliction, anxiety or depression if he is able to abide in non-dual awareness. It is therefore desirable to identify these symptoms and pay attention to them. Neglecting them can increase the difficulties, intensify habits, and thicken the karma. One must also consider serious medical conditions, as neglecting them can be life threatening. A teacher or therapist of non-duality who is not aware of the medical basis of arrhythmia, for example, may interpret it as an anxiety attack. He may then guide the student or the patient to observe these waves of anxiety attacks as they rise and dissipate, and not renounce them but rather meditate on them and rest in non-dual awareness. Such a directive may put the student or the patient in real danger.

Indeed, Prendergast has defined and rated therapists who use non-duality. But from a philosophical point of view, in an unconditional awareness devoid of any reference there can be no degrees of development, judgment or labels. Nothing can be imposed on such a state of mind, neither the decision to be judgmental nor the deliberate shift of the focus of attention to the components of traumatic memory. If so, how can we understand what therapists such as Nixon and Prendergast offer? Furthermore, in the thought and practice of non-duality, means and causes are identical with ends and effects, respectively, otherwise we will find ourselves in a position of duality—between means and ends, between subject and object, between now and then. If so, how do we understand the nature of treatment based on non-duality? After all, the means of treatment are awareness devoid of any preference, and the goal is to cure or find a solution to a certain psychological problem.

American psychologist Sheila Krystal, who is interested in Eastern non-dual doctrines, argues that a therapeutic approach of non-duality cannot promote a method, theory or discourse. At the same time, its point of departure is a discursive activity associated with psychological difficulties. When the therapist and the patient remain with each other in the presence of awareness, the psychological problems break down, lose their conditioning power, and the patient abandons the belief that he has a problem.[30]

The answer to the philosophical difficulties I have raised is clarified through Krystal's own words. Although the answer is partial, at the same time it seems sufficient. Krystal is careful not to fall into the conceptualization of non-duality and to avoid turning it into another ideological mental pattern. Such a mental pattern might provide theoretical reassurance, but at the same time it is a limited framework that distorts reality. Ultimately, the goal of the therapeutic meeting is mental healing that can reduce the suffering of the person and others.

Let us complete the picture by returning to Dzogchen, where one's intrinsic natural awareness is inseparable from the *dharmakāya*, the primary base of the world of phenomena. *Dharmakāya* is beyond any perception and conceptualization. It is beyond time, space and causality, and at the same time exists as an infinite potentiality, a kind of cosmic womb from which phenomena arise, samsaric or nirvanic, just before we name them and give them a sense of concreteness by labeling. In other words, *dharmakāya* is the moment when the natural awareness and the world of preconceptualized phenomena are in a state of integration, in non-duality. Just as the reflections in the mirror are not different from the mirror, there is no duality between the mirror and the objects reflected in it. The mirror is all the reflections, and all the reflections are the mirror.

This integration is central to the therapeutic approach of non-duality. Treatment is a process of continuous reflection in various levels of intensity, a process in which the therapist and the patient stay with each other in a presence of awareness without preferences. This presence reflects with increasing clarity the patient's mental charge or burden as it is, without any involvement or identification, releasing the patient from such a burden.

From a pragmatic point of view, the internal and external phenomena which are endowed with causes of affliction require different approaches, and the choice of approach stems from the patient's mental state. Thus, non-duality and psychotherapy, in a variety of methods, can complement each other. Non-duality is never separate from phenomena. While it is a key to overcoming suffering, many methods of psychotherapy may also help address a variety of psychological problems. The view that non-duality is the only approach to dealing with emotional problems is liable to create another framework that makes a limited and distorted reference to reality. The integration of Eastern and Western methods may be problematic because of their different histories and cultural origins. The attempt to integrate them may lead to the misinterpretation and dilution of their essential ideas. The concept of awareness, for example, is a key concept in Dzogchen that relates to natural and unconditional awareness. It implies a promise, and therefore entices both therapists and patients. But does Nixon's choiceless awareness have the same meaning as the natural awareness of Dzogchen, an awareness of non-duality?

As long as the therapist succeeds in presenting the patient with a mental space devoid of any content or preference, a space in which there is no mental action related to analysis or understanding of anything, there is no fundamental difference between the therapist's and Longchenpa's approaches to such a state of mind. Longchenpa aims to directly introduce natural awareness, the true inner being as a base that has always been there, to which the disciple is exposed without being swept into distracted thinking and behavior. In Dzogchen, the idea of "direct introduction"[31] is of great importance and has special significance. This term marks the moment when the disciple becomes intimately acquainted with the nature of his mind in a decisive experience.[32]

However, if the therapist is not experienced or mature enough to abide in the choiceless awareness and awaken it in the patient, he may confuse this awareness with a calm state of mind, which depends on an object on which all attention is focused. It is then a state of meditation that depends on an object in order to establish itself and is similar to the Dzogchen type of meditation, *zhine* (equivalent to *śamatha* in Sanskrit), one-pointed meditation which includes duality of meditating subject and the object of meditation. In other words, the concentration is on a single object for the purpose of quieting or blocking the mental processes. In the continuation of the meditation practice, the meditation progresses toward the dynamic state of mind, dependent on an object in motion, *lhantong* (Sanskrit: *vipaśyanā*).

In Dzogchen, the concept of natural awareness concerns the unconditional presence of this awareness which exists whether we are peaceful or dynamic. It is a state that is independent of any object, a presence integrated and merged into any activity. It is therefore useful to discern between the awareness of non-duality and object-oriented, static or dynamic meditation. But if in the therapeutic context the dialogue is focused on the purpose of the treatment and the psychological materials brought to the treatment session, the therapeutic session will not differ fundamentally from any other therapeutic session, although it may be defined as a therapeutic approach, based on accessing choiceless or non-dual awareness.

The discussion of yogic psychology, modern psychology and integrated psychology involved with non-duality clarifies the treatment of mental imprints and patterns of behavior, and helps us to understand the outline of Longchenpa's methods. For Dzogchen practitioners, this discussion opens up a field of therapeutic options that will help them remove layers of hidden mental content that dictate and determine their lives, until they acquire enough skills in the method of natural self-release.

Epilogue

The voice of the Keśin, the long-haired yogi, faded and disappeared from abstract thought during the movement between the chapters of the book, which is directed at the real Self, hidden beneath the psychological layers of mind, into the act of yoga psychology. This act occurs in relation to the phenomenal reality immersed in itself. I wondered where the voice had gone. However, as the psychological method developed and formed—not only as a tool for coping with negative thoughts and behaviors, but also for coping with their painful psychological-emotional burden—the yogi's voice is heard again over the horizon, where the basic moral rules of yoga are fulfilled and implemented.

This time it is Patañjali's own voice, indicating the changes that will be made in the environment of the one who fulfills the basic rules of ethics of yoga: there will be no physical, verbal or mental violence in his environment; he will have control over the consequences of his actions; he will have power; he will acquire knowledge of previous births and incarnations; he will gain purity of mind devoid of any attachment or bondage; he will experience joy, one-pointed concentration and control of the senses; he will feel supreme bliss; he will achieve supreme concentration through devotion and surrender to God.[1] These powers are definitely within the reach of Keśin, who is transported by the power of his silent mind on the wind, and who is invisible.

Vyāsa examines violent behavior in its various manifestations, and unlike Patañjali, he notes its consequences for others, both enemy and animal: the offending person will suffer from loss of vitality and numbing of the senses; he will find himself in hell or incarnate as an animal; he will have an incurable disease. Vyāsa further argues that these consequences are also relevant to the violation of other ethical principles, such as theft and the denial of truth.

The words of Vyāsa and Patañjali imply that there is a kind of personal system of reward and punishment, and the very existence of such a system can encourage behavior that does not violate the moral principles of yoga. But this will not be for the right reason. The method of *Pratipakṣa bhāvanā* helps to realize these principles and supports them, not out of desire for achievement or fear of the consequences of their violation, but rather because it is the practice of the opposite. It is based not only on consistent and repetitive practice (*abhyāsa*), but also on uninvolved awareness (*vairāgya*) toward liberation from *avidyā*, ignorance. The practice of *vairāgya* is rooted in non-attachment to gain and loss, to hope and fear.

This form of dispassion or uninvolved awareness directs the practitioner toward the realization of these principles with the understanding of what is the right or appropriate thing to do in a given circumstance. Moreover, the fulfilment of these principles is a complete necessity, an ultimate vow, that must be fulfilled regardless of place, time, circumstances, socioeconomic or social status, or the caste to which the practitioner belongs.[2] Therefore, practitioners who have chosen a yogic way of life see these principles as universal. For Patañjali, the observance of these principles is the great vow. These principles are neither negotiable nor flexible, nor influenced by modern interpretations of the *Yoga Sūtras* or social ideologies. This static approach reflects the interpretation of scholars such as Bryant and Feuerstein, who believe that Patañjali's approach to the great vow is decisive and final.

Unlike them, I wonder whether it is time to formulate a dynamic approach in which the static understanding of Patañjali's moral principles will serve only as a basis from which we may uncover the hidden meanings of these principles and extract new insights from them. Such a dynamic approach could be adopted when approaching Indian texts such as the Bhagavad Gītā, where the moral principle of non-violence is not absolute, but depends on the caste of the yogi and the duties that derive from his social position. It may also relate to the yogic-tantric texts which, under certain conditions, permit sexual intercourse and the eating of meat and fish, or to the Western moral philosophies based on aspects of moral relativism, utilitarianism and moral egotism. Such a dynamic approach opens up new possibilities for future research. For the twenty-first century practitioner, this research may shed light on Patañjali's ultimate vow.

Patañjali's message about the absolute necessity of fulfilling the principles of yoga ethics is not essentially altruistic and focused on the well-being of others. It is a condition for one's liberation from the chains of the *avidyā*. Liberation involves the fulfillment of these principles in interactions with others. Liberation is part of one's responsibility to others and cannot be realized without realizing these moral principles. In this way, the relationship between yogic liberation and society as a whole forms the basis of a moral system.

The purpose of the practice of cultivating the opposite is only to realize the yogi's moral principles for their own sake, since they are the natural expression of liberation from the bonds of ignorance. The practice has no other purpose and is not intended to attain special yogic powers, mental or physical needs, or to avoid dealing with situations involving suffering and pain. If the practitioner tries to achieve such goals while not being sufficiently skilled in uninvolved awareness, he may continue to inflame the causes of affliction.

Cultivating the opposite on the way to realizing the ethical principles of yoga enables the dormant mental imprints etched in the mind to be diluted and weakened, thus dismantling the causes of affliction from their conditioned emotional reactions. The fruits of this practice, including a nonviolent environment, control over the consequences of one's actions, knowledge of births and incarnations, one-pointed concentration, control of the senses and bliss, are only the means to reducing the pain and suffering of the yogi and others on the way to yoga. They are not an end in themselves.

My observations of the psychological *pratipakṣa bhāvanā* point to a foundation for revealing new meaning for the practitioner. I believe that the practice of the opposite, the *pratipakṣa bhāvanā*, is a combination of imagining and thinking about the consequences of thoughts and actions that violate the principles of yogic morality. The process generates self-honesty, sensitivity and closeness to others in an emphatic sense, and remorse along with an inquiry regarding the motives underlying these thoughts and actions. This combination allows for a double process that combines well with yoga practice, one based on *abhyāsa*, a repetitive practice, and the other based on *vairāgya*, an involved awareness of dispassion.

Longchenpa's practice also stimulates a wide range of thoughts and feelings that are usually held captive in the mind. Exposing them enables the practitioner to empty his mind of them, to express them uncontrolled to the point of exhaustion to reduce their emotional burden. Exhaustion weakens his defenses. Immediately afterwards, the practitioner observes these emotions and thoughts without attempting to suppress or block them. He simply recognizes and acknowledges them. He must refrain from engaging in an internal discourse about them, and from being trapped in them. Then they will be released on their own, and this release enables the dilution of the potential of mental imprints and helps to break down the causes of affliction from their charge.

The purpose of such a practice is to allow the dawning of the practitioner's inherent natural awareness once the causes of affliction have been dismantled of their activating emotional charge. On the way to this fulfillment, the practitioner will achieve a profoundly healing mental change, albeit temporarily: a reduction in the emotional burden accompanied with healing and liberating insight.

If so, Patañjali's practice of the opposite and Longchenpa's cathartic practice are powerful and effective, and eventually they will be able to decompose the *kleśas* from their emotional burden. However, the completion of these exercises and their actual application may take a very long time, even for incarnations, and the practitioner may encounter many difficulties, especially when he encounters stubborn and compulsive *kleśas*. Moreover, even when the practice of yoga and meditation touch the spiritual heights, mental imprints continue to exist. They are like subterranean currents, which may surface at any moment in the face of any stimulus, ready to be triggered and expressed into patterns of behavior and causes of affliction.

In addition, sometimes the practice itself can serve as a spiritual bypass, an evasion from real and direct confrontation with emotions, relationships, and the demands of phenomenal existence. Therefore, one cannot avoid asking: What will the practitioner do until then, in light of patterns of behavior that repeatedly cause pain to himself and his surroundings? What will he do in the face of patterns that prevent him from moving toward personal growth, toward harmonious relationships with his family, his friends and his community, and toward the realization of yoga?

Western psychology offers a variety of methods to deal with the difficulties that may complement the practice of the opposite and cathartic practice. The work of Robert Miller presents one method that addresses impulsive-compulsive disorders and helps to resolve situations of stress, trauma, anxiety and compulsive behavior. Through Miller's method, it is possible to clearly identify the mental imprints, the patterns of behavior and the causes of affliction, and to help the yoga practitioner relieve the causes of affliction of their intense emotional burden.

Surprisingly, Miller's therapeutic process does not rely on strategies to dismantle the compulsive behavior of its activating power. The patient is not required to refrain from completely avoiding the object to which his compulsive behavior is intended, such as gambling. The therapeutic process allows the patient to come into contact and engage with the object of desire while simultaneously neutralizing and releasing the compulsiveness associated with it.

If so, yoga practitioners, like religious followers who are limited by religious or moral vows or injunctions, may be helped by the practices of opposite and of catharsis to remove layers of hidden mental content that dictate and modulate their lives, and at the same time they can turn to certain methods in Western psychology as a temporary and supplemental treatment option.

Glossary

abhiniveśa: clinging to life or fear of death; one of the five **kleśas**.

abhyāsa: repetitive practice; cultivating a discipline of practice. Yoga practice consists of two foundational components implemented simultaneously: **abhyāsa** and **vairāgya**, repetitiveness and dispassion.

Advaita-Vedānta: a philosophical school mostly associated with the great eighth-century Indian philosopher and teacher Śaṅkara. Its core tenet is that of a singularity as a unitary metaphysical essence (Brahman) that underlies and precedes multiplicity, the world of phenomena, where the individual's real Self (Ātman) and that unitary metaphysical essence (Brahman) are identical, being a non-duality.

Advaitin: a follower of **Advaita-Vedānta.**

ahiṃsā: non-harming; non-violence. One of the **yamas**.

asmitā: "sense of I-am-ness," that in its initial form, **asmitā,** stands for sentience of pure awareness reflected in the mind. It stands as the agent for the power of seeing or perceiving involved in the world distinct from the principle of inactive and uninvolved pure awareness (**puruṣa**). **Asmitā** is the agent, the empirical or phenomenal self that depends on the senses to perceive and cognize. It solidifies further when in contact with sense objects—tangible or intangible—grasps them, and refers to them with a sense of identification and ownership. Everything the ego knows, feels and acts is known to itself as his own ("my pleasure") or identified with ("I am angry"). This sense of ownership or identification differentiates the individual as a separate unique being, defined by personal boundaries. As such, **asmitā** is one of the five **kleśas.**

aṣṭāṅga-yoga: the eight limbs of yoga, consisting of **yama, niyama, āsana, prāṇāyāma, pratyāhāra, dhāraṇā, dhyāna** and **samādhi**.

avidyā: fundamental ignorance of one's inherent true Self that consists of a mundane phenomenal perspective through which one is involved in the world. Such perspective conceals the principle of pure awareness and "covers" it by establishing a false identity, the sense of the ego that distorts perceptions of reality. As such, it is one of the five **kleśas** and the base for the other four.

Atiyoga: is mentioned in an eighth-century Indic tantra text called *Sarvabuddhasamāyoga*,[1] signifying utmost yoga in which one's true nature is fully experienced as the culmination of the meditative practice of deity yoga (the visualization of a deity and recitation of his or her mantra). In the tenth century, Atiyoga was identified as a separate spiritual path. According to ninth-century Tibetan scholar Nubchen Yeshe, the doctrine of Atiyoga "is the best and utmost Yoga, the mother of all conquerors, its name is **Dzogchen** because it gives detailed teaching with a view of imparting direct understanding of the principal of non-sought spontaneity with regard to all existential elements."[2] Here, spontaneity means an unpremeditated or unplanned response to an event or an object, unmediated or conditioned by concepts or mental constructs that occur in the mind experienced within self-awareness.

bag chags: (in Tibetan, which is similar to the term **vāsanā** in Sanskrit), meaning "a pattern of behavior" or "habitual tendency," the organization of latent mental imprints into configured units that turn into patterns of behavior and character.

Bhagavad Gītā: The poem of the Lord, a 700-verse Hindu scripture that dates from the fifth century to the second century BCE, and is set in a narrative framework of a dialogue between Pandava prince Arjuna and his guide and charioteer lord Kṛṣṇa. It significantly covers various branches of yoga and ideas from **Sāṅkhya** philosophy.

bhāṣya: commentary; primary commentary based on the root text.

buddhi: the faculty or seat of intelligence; the intellect dominated by **sattva**.

citi: pure mind, empty (not in the sense of nihilism) of content or object, tangible or intangible.

citi-śakti: the power of pure mind as potentiality.

citta: complex structure of all of the mental and physical functions of the mind. It is the axis around which the **Yogasūtra** revolves.

citta-vṛtti: mental activity or mental processes. For Patañjali, yoga is the cessation of mental processes; stillness of mind.

dhāraṇā: the very beginning of meditation where one concentrates and places his attention on a single point. One of the eight limbs of yoga.

dharmakāya: within the context of Dzogchen, it literally means the "Buddha reality body"; that is to say, the world of phenomena and the existence in such a world as it is. It refers to the essential potentiality of the world of phenomena, a time before it appears as a solid form and before it is objectified and sorted out by the individual perception. This preconceptual form of perception points to the prior relationship that exists between one's essential nature of mind and the ground of its origination as the dharmakāya. As such it conveys an experience of inseparability or non-duality between the two. Dharmakāya stands for the world of phenomena as it is, before being conceptualized or labeled by the individual, hence it is seen clearly as it is.

dhyāna: an advanced stage of meditation in which one is able to concentrate and to maintain one single train of thought for long durations without being distracted. One of the eight limbs of yoga.

duḥkha: suffering; pain; a condition in which one is confronted by thoughts, feelings, sensations and situations one would prefer not to experience, or a condition where one is confronted by separation from one's loved ones, and from pleasant and joyful experiences which one would prefer not to experience.

Dzogchen: (Tibetan) literally, "Great Perfection." A transmission of teachings in Tibetan Buddhism aimed at discovering one's inherent natural awareness and continuing to abide in that natural primordial awareness or state of being. Dzogchen is an important stream of teachings within the **Nyingma** school of Tibetan Buddhism.

guṇa: a quality or dynamic force (as opposed to a potential one). There are three qualities that describe the manner in which activity is generated and takes place in **prakṛti** or in the world of phenomena. The three guṇas are **sattva**, **rajas** and **tamas,** and yoga is about their cessation or stoppage.

haṭha-yoga: force or power; a branch of yoga which is primarily concerned with postures and breath. The **haṭha-yoga** literature consists of the Haṭhayogapradīpikā (dated fourteenth or fifteenth century CE).

kaivalya: aloneness; aloofness; freedom; a state in which the mental processes are brought to complete cessation and pure awareness, and **puruṣa,** the real Self or one's metaphysical core Selfhood, is isolated and disengaged from its confusing entanglement with **prakṛti**, the world of phenomena.

karma: literally denotes action and refers to results of given actions. Such results leave "traces" that will be the seed beds that later will germinate and shape one's future circumstances. It is a vicious cycle of causes and their effects, of which a yogi attempts to extricate himself.

Keśin: the archetypal yogic figure of Vedic culture; the long-haired ascetic wanderer with mystical powers who lives in the forest, far from any social framework.

kevala-kumbhaka: a suspended breathing that occurs abruptly, by itself, and in accordance with an intense meditative concentration (**samādhi**) enabling the dawn of discerning insight (**vivekakhyāti**) and supernatural powers.

kleśa: "cause of affliction"; psychological dispositions through which one interacts and reacts to the world of phenomena causing himself and others harm, pain or stress. The five **kleśas** are **avidyā**, **asmitā**, **rāga** (attraction), **dveṣa** (aversion) and **abhiniveśa.**

Lhatong: (Tibetan term which is similar to the term **vipaśyanā** in Sanskrit) in the context of Dzogchen, it means that one remains in mental stillness despite the occurring mental movements or fluctuation, without being distracted. This state is achieved by a meditation as a fixation without an object by which the practitioner becomes familiar with the movement of thoughts, but without being distracted by it. If by **zhine**, meditatively fixating pointedly on an object, one achieves a calm state of mind. By Lhatong, the practitioner meditatively fixates without object, such as sky gazing or gazing at a random point in space, and one is able to familiarize oneself with the mental movements while maintaining stillness. In fact, it is a state in which "calmness," encountered while fixating on an object, and "movement"; that is, the arising of thoughts, coexist simultaneously.

mahā-vratam: the ultimate vow to observe the ethical principles of yoga independently of place, time and circumstances.

manas: the faculty of mind that recognises, receives and sorts sense data from the world of phenomena.

nirodha: cessation, stoppage or suspension, referring to the mental processes.

nirodha saṃskāras: a type of mental imprints that when activated they intensify the control of mental processes and make them still.

nirvāṇa: literally "blown out," or the shutting down or extinction of all burning desires that perpetuate one's accumulation of karma, which represents the ultimate state of liberation from **saṃsāra**, or freedom.

niyama: niyama: observances of ethical guidelines. There are five niyamas: *śauca* - internal and external yogic cleansing; *saṃtoṣa* – contentment; *tapas* - austerities or practices involved with inner heat; *svādhyāya* - daily recitation or study of texts; and *īśvara-praṇidhāna* - devotion to the lord or deity.

Nyingma: (Tibetan) literally means "ancient'"; the oldest of the four major schools of Tibetan Buddhism. It is also considered as the school of the "ancient [first] translations of Buddhist scriptures" from Sanskrit into Tibetan in the eighth century. The Nyingma tradition actually comprises several distinct lineages that all trace their origins to the Indian master Padmasamhava. Traditionally, Nyingma was constituted of a loose network of lay practitioners, while monasteries inhabited by monks and nuns assimilated with the practice of reincarnated spiritual masters.

pariṇāma: transformations or evolutionary processes that occur in the world of phenomena as the constant changes that characterize relative reality.

prajñā: yogic insight or wisdom that occurs when in meditative absorption, bypassing perception, reasoning and reliable testimony. Yogic insight means knowing something new about a certain object we did not know before, toward seeing the object "as it is."

prakṛti: the perceptible and imperceptible dimensions of the world of phenomena, events and conditioned existence. Prakṛti and **puruṣa** (one's metaphysical core Selfhood) are radically different. Against our intuition, our mind, and its mental processes, our psychological makeup and its feelings and emotions, as well as our yoga practice, all are considered components of prakṛti.

prāṇāyāma: breath control, or more precisely control of one's **prāṇā**: vital energy. As the mind is linked and bound with breath, practicing breath retention enhances mental pacification.

pratyāhāra: withdrawal of the senses. It is concerned with the disengagement from sense object, because contact with sense objects can trigger or ignite mental processes as reactions to the object. For me, it is the disengagement from the mental processes that are triggered or ignited when coming in contact with a sense object, not from the sense-object in itself.

Pratyāhāra: the fifth of the eight limbs of yoga.

puruṣa: core of Selfhood or the principle of pure inherent awareness; completely different from one's physical existence, including one's biological, mental and psychological components of **prakṛti.** According to Patañjali, there is a multiplicity of puruṣas.

rajas: one of the three **guṇas**, or dynamic forces (as opposed to a potential one) that generate activity in **prakṛti,** the world of phenomena, that is responsible for activities generated by vigor, heat and passion.

rigpa: (Tibetan) in context, Dzogchen means "awareness" (which is similar to the term *vidyā* in Sanskrit) and refers to pristine cognition as the essential nature of mind. It is the self-presented principle of intelligence in its pure and undiluted intensity, which enables perception of physical and psychic elements and events. It is a pristine cognition of sense objects, in the sense that it occurs directly, without the mediation of concepts, language, symbols or any other means. This principle in its pure essence is inherent within individuals as their true "nature of mind," their natural awareness, or Buddha nature. This stands in contrast with the individual's ordinary compulsive mental processes or events of the "ordinary mind." Abiding in the undistorted nature of mind refers to the natural state of presence.

sādhana: practice applied on the path to liberation from ignorance (**avidyā**) and suffering (**duḥkha**).

śakti: power; energy; capacity; potency.

samādhi: concentration; steadfast meditative absorption as an enstasy in which the yogi withdraws from mental activity. It is first established when the object of meditation alone shines forth as if the mind is empty of its subjective essence or any other content (except the object of meditation itself). It continues being established until it is completely steady and independent of any object of meditation, which means that the yogi is liberated.

saṃsāra: wandering or transmigration referring to the cycle of death and rebirth or reincarnation, and to the aimless wandering in mundane existence caused by karma from which yogis aspire to extricate themselves and to become liberated. It is a fundamental belief of most Indian schools of philosophy, including Buddhism.

saṃskāra: dormant mental imprint etched in one's mind in reaction to events, conditions and sense objects that construct psychological content, including self-perception, that determines the manner in which one interacts with the world. Such dormant mental imprints in certain circumstances have the potential to instigate and generate mental and physical actions.

saṃyama: yogic meditation in which **dhāraṇā**, **dhyāna** and **samādhi** are applied together.

Sāṃkhya: probably the earliest school of thought of Indian philosophy which discerns between **puruṣa** and **prakṛti**, the metaphysical core Selfhood and the world of phenomena, and describes the latter as an evolutionary process from the subtlest realms of the mind to the concrete reality of objects, events and activities; based on the elements earth, water, fire, air and space.

sattva: one of the three **guṇas**, dynamic forces that generate states of mind characterized by clarity, lucidity, purity, transparency and peace.

siddhi: yogic accomplishment; special forces beyond ordinary capacities the yogi obtains as a result of a meditation directed to specific objects either related with one's body, one's subtle body or yogic ethics. The achievement of such "miraculous" forces that can generate wisdom and enable the yogi to assist others is a mark of skilful yogi. The yogi can be fascinated, entangled and consumed by such powers.

svādhyāya: recitation of mantras and study of texts by oneself, leading to purification or to liberation. Such a study implies self-reflection as well.

svarūpa: original independent essence as **puruṣa,** inherent in people.

tamas: darkness; heaviness; one of the three **guṇas**, characterized by inertia, fatigue and passivity.

tapas: austerities or yogic practice that generate heat that burns the yogi's impurities.

Upaniṣads: the ancient Sanskrit texts of spiritual teaching and ideas of Hinduism that deal with meditation, philosophy and spiritual knowledge that revolve around the identity; composed from 800 to 300 BCE. **Advaita-Vedānta** traces its roots to the **Upaniṣads**.

vairāgya: dispassion toward or uninvolved awareness of the objective world. Yoga practice consists of two foundational components implemented simultaneously, of **abhyāsa** and **vairāgya**, repetitiveness and dispassion respectively. For example, in performing a posture, the practitioner performs it for the sake of it without being envious of how another practitioner in the studio performs that posture, without competing with him. Here envy implies that the practitioner lacks something that he desires which enhances distractive mental activity.

Vajrayāna: translated as "Diamond Vehicle"; refers to the various Buddhist traditions of tantra and "secret mantra," which developed in India in the seventh century and spread to Tibet and Bhutan, and included practices that employ mantras, mandalas (mystical diagrams), and visualizations of deities.

vāsanā: a pattern of thinking and behaving, which together with **kleśas** and **saṃskāras**, consist of one's psychological framework that dictates one's existence.

Vedas: literally, knowledge; a large body of religious Sanskrit texts originating in ancient India. They are considered revelations heard by ancient sages after intense meditation, consisting of hymns dedicated to deities that entail rituals, mantras ceremonies and sacrifices.

vikalpa: verbal construction; a conceptualization, as mental activity is unable to describe precisely and inform of subtle states of mind, particularly to portray **puruṣa**.

viveka-khyāti: yogic discernment between **prakṛti** and **puruṣa** that occurs in the culmination of cognitive object-based **samādhi.** In that steadfast meditative absorption, the object of meditation, "sense of I-am-ness" (**asmitā**) alone shines forth as if the mind is empty of its subjective essence or any other content (except the object of meditation itself). The yogi then understands that the sense of I-am-ness, a component of **prakṛti**, as his personality is not **puruṣa**, the real Self. **Viveka-khyāti** is the key to liberation of entanglement with the world of phenomena.

vṛtti: process; activity; fluctuation.

vyutthāna saṃskāras: a type of mental imprint; when activated they force the mind to direct the gaze outward at sensory objects, like a magnet attracted by metal objects. They perpetuate a distorted perception of reality and cause the pain and suffering that perpetuates conditioned existence.

yama: principal yogic ethical guideline; restraint. There are five yamas: *ahiṃsā* - nonviolence; *satya* - truthfulness, radical honesty; *asteya* - non-stealing; *brahmacarya* – celibacy; and *aparigraha* - non-possessivenss.

Yoga: Patañjali is very clear and firm in his definition of yoga as the cessation of mental activity, which is different from the widespread view is yoga as union of body and mind. But the mind and body belong to the domain of **prakṛti**, already inseparably connected. Also, it is not exactly a union between the pure subject, the real Self, and the world of sense objects, **prakṛti** or the union of the true Self as the principle of awareness and the body, but rather, yoga starts with the realization of their radical difference. Yoga as a union occurs when the principle of pure awareness, or true Self, is realized by means of meditation that stills and empties the mind of mental processes. Then the true Self dawns and goes back to abide in its true nature and unites with the aggregated, all-embracing Selfhood.

Yoga Sūtras: the aphorisms or the verses of yoga.

Zhine: (Tibetan term which is similar to the term *śamatha* in Sanskrit) refers to calm state of mind culminating in contentless state of mind, achieved by practicing single-pointed meditation.

Notes

Introduction

1. J. Engler, "Promises and Perils of the Spiritual Path," in M. Unno, ed., *Buddhism and Psychotherapy Across Cultures* (Boston, MA: Wisdom Publications, 2006).
2. Ibid., p. 23.
3. K. Werner, "Yoga and the Ṛg Veda: An Interpretation of the Keśin Hymn (RV 10, 136)," *Religious Studies*, vol. 13, no. 3 (September 1977), pp. 289–302.
4. Ibid.
5. T. S. Eliot, *Four Quartets* (London: Faber & Faber, 2001 [1941]), p. 4.
6. J. Welwood, *Toward a Psychology of Awakening: Buddhism, Psychotherapy, and the Path of Personal and Spiritual Transformation* (Boston, MA: Shambhala, 2000), p. 11.
7. "For one who has discrimination, everything is suffering on account of the suffering produced by the consequences [of action], by pain [itself], and by the *saṁskāras*, as well as on account of the suffering ensuing from the turmoil of the *vṛttis* due to the *guṇas*." *Sūtra* 2.15, E. F. Bryant, *The Yoga Sūtras of Patañjali: A New Edition, Translation and Commentary* (New York: North Point Press, 2009), p. 203.
8. W. Halbfass, *Tradition and Reflection: Explorations in Indian Thought* (New York: State University of New York Press, 1991), p. 244.
9. "The conjunction between the seer and that which is seen is the cause [of suffering] to be avoided." *Sūtra* 2.17, Bryant, *The Yoga Sūtras of Patañjali*, p. 213.
10. "The means to liberation is uninterrupted discriminative discernment." *Sūtra* 2.26, Bryant, *The Yoga Sūtras of Patañjali*, p. 234.
11. "The fourth [prāṇāyāma] surpasses the sphere of both the external and internal [prāṇāyāma]." *Sūtra* 2.51, T. S. Rukmani, trans. and ed., *Yogavārttika of Vijñānabhikṣu: Samādhipāda*, vol. 2 (Delhi: Munshiram Manoharlal Publishers, 2007), pp. 228–229.

12. In the yoga tradition there is ample evidence of yogis holding their breath for a long time. See a collection of such testimonies in Bryant, *The Yoga Sūtras of Patañjali*, p. 293.
13. "When that is accomplished, the seer abides in its own true nature." *Sūtra* 1.3, Bryant, *The Yoga Sūtras of Patañjali*, p. 22.
14. C. K. Chapple and A. L. Funes Maderey (eds.), *Thinking with the Yoga Sūtra of Patañjali: Translation and Interpretation* (London: Lexington Books, 2019), p. xii.
15. *Sūtra* 2.34, ibid., p. 257.

Chapter 1

1. G. Feuerstein, *The Philosophy of Classical Yoga* (Rochester, VT: Inner Traditions, 1996), p. 58.
2. U. Arya, *Yoga-sūtras of Patañjali with the Exposition of Vyasa: A Translation and Commentary, Volume I—Samādhi-pāda* (Honesdale, PA: Himalayan Institute Press, 1986), p. 452.
3. *Sūtra* 1.2, Bryant, *The Yoga Sūtras of Patañjali*, p. 10.
4. *Sūtra* 1.38: "The mind-field whose object in meditation is the observation, awareness and knowledge of the dream or sleep states become stabilised." Arya, *Yoga-sūtras of Patañjali*, p. 361.
5. For further reading on the topic, see Namkhai Norbu, *The Cycle of Day and Night*, trans. J. Reynolds (Barrytown, NY: Station Hill Press, 2000).
6. *Sūtra* 1.2, D. Raveh, *Exploring the Yogasūtra: Philosophy and Translation*, annotated edition (London: Continuum), p. 127.
7. One of the earliest schools associated with history of yoga philosophy provides yoga with a metaphysical framework, which enumerates the elements that constitute the world of phenomena, and their separation from the principle of pure awareness through philosophical reasoning and study. The goal of this school of thought is to lead to an understanding of the underlying truth of ultimate reality.
8. "Through *saṃyama* on that, or by omens (*ariṣṭa*), foreknowledge of death is obtained." *Sūtra* 3.23, Raveh, *Exploring the Yogasūtra*, p. 134.
9. Feuerstein, *The Philosophy of Classical Yoga*, p. 75.
10. N. Norbu, *Dream Yoga and the Practice of Natural Light* (New York: Snow Lion, 2002), p. 22.
11. Raveh, *Exploring the Yogasūtra*, p. 77.
12. Y. Grinshpon, *Silence and Liberation in Classical Yoga* (Tel Aviv: Ministry of Defense, Israel, 2002), pp. 12–13 (in Hebrew).

13. I. Whicher, "Cessation and Integration in Classical Yoga," *Asian Philosophy*, vol. 5, no. 1 (1995), p. 47.
14. Raveh, *Exploring the Yogasūtra*, p. 84.
15. J. Krishnamurti, *Freedom from the Known* (San Francisco, CA: Harper, 2009), p. 35.
16. The nouns "mauni" and "maunya" are derived from the root "man," which means "thinking," "meditating," "meditating in silence." Over time, new meanings were added to these words such as "silent," "vow of silence," and "silence." It seems that long-hair's achievements in meditation are similar to that of the classical yogi, and the difference is only in terminology. After all, there are two texts, the *Rig-Veda* and the *Yoga Sūtras*, written at least a millennium apart. See Werner, "Yoga and the Ṛg Veda," p. 293.
17. A few prominent scholars have translated *smṛti* in the context of *sūtra* 1.20 not as "memory" but as "intentness." See Arya, *Yoga-sūtras of Patañjali*, p. 224. Raveh uses the term "mindfulness" (*Exploring the Yogasūtra*, p. 127), as does G. Feuerstein, *The Yoga-Sūtra of Patañjali: A New Translation and Commentary* (Rochester, VT: Inner Traditions, 1989), p. 40; and "attention" is used by F. Tola and C. Dragonetti, *The Yogasūtras of Patañjali on Concentration of Mind*, trans. K. D. Prithipaul (India: Motilal Banarsidass, 1955), p. 71.
18. A. Miller, *The Drama of the Gifted Child: The Search for the True Self* (Tel Aviv: Dvir, 1992), p. 28. (Hebrew).
19. Raveh, *Exploring the Yogasūtra*, p. 130.
20. Feuerstein, *The Yoga-Sūtra of Patañjali*, p. 62.
21. Raveh, *Exploring the Yogasūtra*, p. 130.
22. M. Jakubczak, "The Sense of Ego-maker in Classical Sāṃkhya and Yoga: Reconsideration of Ahaṃkāra," *Cracow Indological Studies*, vol. 10 (2008), p. 42.
23. D. Raveh, *Philosophical Threads in Patañjali's Yoga* (Tel Aviv: Hakibutz Hameuchad, 2010), p. 84 (in Hebrew).
24. C. Trungpa, *Cutting Through Spiritual Materialism* (Boston, MA: Shambhala, 1987), p. 22.
25. G. Ifergan, *The Man from Samye: Longchenpa on Praxis, Its Negation and Liberation* (New Delhi: Aditya Prakashan, 2014), pp. 133–134.
26. Bryant, *The Yoga Sūtras of Patañjali*, p. 191.
27. Ibid., p. 176.
28. H. Āraṇya, *Yoga Philosophy of Patañjali: Containing his Yoga Aphorisms with Vyāsa's Commentary in Original Sanskrit and Annotations Thereon with Copious*

Hints on the Practice of Yoga (India: Calcutta University Press, 1981), pp. 117–118.

29. P. Olivelle, trans., *The Early Upaniṣads* (Delhi: Oxford University Press, 1998), p. 121.
30. N. Mishra, "Saṁskāras in Yoga Philosophy and Western Psychology," *Philosophy East and West*, vol. 2, no. 4 (1953), p. 308.
31. G. Feuerstein, *Encyclopedic Dictionary of Yoga* (Saint Paul, MN: Paragon House,1990), p. 309.
32. Mishra, "Saṁskāras in Yoga Philosophy and Western Psychology," p. 314.
33. Raveh, *Philosophical Threads*, p. 101.
34. C. Dickens, *A Christmas Carol and Other Christmas Writings* (London: Penguin 2003 [1843]), p. 35.
35. See also *sūtras* 3.9 and 3.10. in Raveh, *Philosophical Threads*, pp. 224–225.
36. Arya, *Yoga-Sūtras of Patañjali*, p. 419.
37. Āraṇya, *Yoga Philosophy of Patañjali*, p. 108.
38. Ibid.
39. Rukmani, *Yogavārttika of Vijñānabhikṣu: Samādhipāda*, p. 251.
40. Feuerstein, *The Yoga-Sūtra of Patañjali*, p. 57.
41. Y. Grinshpon, personal conversation, 2016.
42. Arya, *Yoga-Sūtras of Patañjali*, p. 419.
43. I. Whicher, "The Liberating Role of Samskāra in Classical Yoga," *Journal of Indian Philosophy*, vol. 33, no. 5 (2005), p. 608.
44. Feuerstein, *The Philosophy of Classical Yoga*, p. 66.
45. Ibid.

Chapter 2

1. "*Kaivalya* is the turning back of the *guṇas* to their source, once [their work] for the sake of *puruṣa* is accomplished; or, it is the power of pure consciousness (*citi-śakti*) abiding in its own essence." Raveh, *Exploring the Yogasūtra*, p. 139.
2. Ibid., p. 130.
3. Āraṇya, *Yoga Philosophy of Patañjali*, p. 129.
4. Bryant, *The Yoga Sūtras of Patañjali*, p. 193.
5. R. Mehta, *Yoga: The Art of Integration: A Commentary on the Yoga Sūtras of Patañjali* (India: The Theosophical Publishing House, 1990), pp. 115–116.
6. "*Dhyāna* is even now of consciousness [in the course of *dhāraṇā*] toward [the object meditated upon]." *Sūtras* 3.2, Raveh, *Exploring the Yogasūtra*, p. 133.

7. Raveh, *Philosophical Threads in Patañjali's Yoga*, p. 221.
8. Retrieved from http://bodhiprinciple.com/practice-pratipaksha-bhāvanā.
9. J. Wood, W. E. Perunovic and J. Lee, "Positive Self-Statements: Power for Some, Peril for Others," *Psychological Science*, vol. 20, no. 7 (2009), p. 860.
10. S. Henshaw, "Why Positive Affirmations Don't Work," *Psych Central*, 2015, https://psychcentral.com.
11. R. S. Mishra, *The Textbook of Yoga Psychology: The Definitive Translation and Interpretation of Patañjali's Yoga Sūtras* (New York: Baba Bhagavandas Publication Trust, 1997), pp. 203–204.
12. R. M. W. Wenzlaff and D. M. Wegner, "Thought Suppression," *Annual Review of Psychology*, vol. 51, 2000, pp. 59–91.
13. Ibid., p. 59.
14. Ibid., p. 60.
15. Ibid., p. 75.
16. P. Booth, "Emotional Disclosure and Psychoneuroimmunology," in K. Vedhara and M. Irwin, eds., *Human Psychoneuroimmunology* (Oxford: Oxford University Press, 2005), p. 319.
17. B. Azar, "A New Take on Psychoneuroimmunology," *Monitor on Psychology*, vol. 32, no. 11, p. 35.
18. Wenzlaff and Wegner, "Thought Suppression," p. 77.
19. J. Welwood, "Embodying Your Realization: Psychological Work in the Service of Spiritual Development," 1999, retrieved from www.johnwelwood.com.
20. Raveh, *Exploring the Yogasūtra*, p. 129.
21. Welwood, "Embodying Your Realization," pp. 4–5.
22. Karen Horney (1885–1952) was a Freudian psychoanalyst who was also an outspoken critic of Freud. She describes the possible characteristics of such a character in her book *Our Inner Conflicts: A Constructive Theory of Neurosis* (New York: W.W. Norton, 1992 [1945]).
23. Feuerstein, *The Yoga-Sūtra of Patañjali*, pp. 82–83.
24. Ibid.
25. Mehta, *Yoga: The Art of Integration*, p. 157.
26. Bryant, *The Yoga Sūtras of Patañjali*, p. 256.
27. Raveh, *Exploring the Yogasūtra*, p. 132.
28. Āraṇya, *Yoga Philosophy of Patañjali*, p. 216.
29. Ibid., p. 218.
30. S. Columba, "The Desert Fathers on Radical Self-Honesty," *Vox Benedictina*, vol. 8. no. 1 (1991), p. 8.

31. See Paul Bloom's work: *Against Empathy: The Case for Rational Compassion* (London: Bodley Head, 2016).
32. Ibid., p. 17.
33. Ibid., p. 18.
34. M. Proeve and S. Tudor, *Remorse: Psychological and Jurisprudential Perspectives* (Abingdon: Routledge, 2010), p. 31.
35. Āraṇya, *Yoga Philosophy of Patañjali*, p. 218.
36. Proeve and Tudor, *Remorse*, p. 43.
37. Raveh, *Exploring the Yogasūtra*, p. 127, *sūtras* 1.11.
38. Bryant, *The Yoga Sūtras of Patañjali*, p. 52.
39. Sūtra 2.46, Raveh, *Exploring the Yogasūtra*, p. 132.

Chapter 3

1. M. Williams, *A Sanskrit–English Dictionary Etymologically and Philologically Arranged with Special Reference to Cognate Indo-European Languages* (Varanasi: Indica, 1996), p. 755.
2. D. Shulman, *More than Real: A History of the Imagination in South India* (Cambridge, MA: Harvard University Press, 2012).
3. Ibid., p. 19.
4. Ibid., pp. 118–119.
5. Ibid., p. 120.
6. K. Csaba, "The Matsyendrasaṃhitā: A yoginī-Centered 13th-Century Yoga Text of the South Indian Śāmbhava Cult," in D. Lorenzen and A. Muñoz, eds., *Yogi Heroes and Poets: Histories and legends of the Nāths* (Albany, NY: SUNY Press, 2011).
7. Ibid., p. 160.
8. D. G. White, *The Yoga Sūtra of Patañjali: A Biography* (Princeton, NJ: Princeton University Press, 2014), p. 26.
9. Shulman, *More than Real*, p.135.
10. *Sūtra* 2.16, Raveh, *Exploring the Yogasūtra*, p. 130.
11. *Sūtra* 2.34, Raveh, *Exploring the Yogasūtra*, p. 132.
12. J. H. Berke, "Shame and Envy," *British Journal of Psychotherapy*, vol 2, no. 4 (1986), p. 263.
13. M. Klein, *Envy and Gratitude, and Other Works, 1946–1963* (New York: Free Press, 1984), p. 181.
14. M. C. Harrison, "The Paradox of Fiction and the Ethics of Empathy: Reconceiving Dickens's Realism," *Narrative*, vol. 16, no. 3 (2008), p. 263.

15. J. H. Clarke, "The Metapsychology of Character Change: A Case Study of Ebenezer Scrooge," *Journal of Spirituality in Mental Health*, vol. 11, no 4 (2009), p. 252.
16. Arya, *Yoga-Sūtras of Patañjali*, p. 63.
17. Bryant, *The Yoga Sūtras of Patañjali*, p. 5.
18. Y. Grinshpon, *Silence Unheard: Deathly Otherness in Patañjali-Yoga* (Albany, NY: State University of New York Press, 2001), p. 17.
19. *Sūtra* 2.48, Raveh, *Exploring the Yogasūtra*, p. 132.
20. *Sūtra* 2.46, ibid.

Chapter 4

1. "It is firmly grounded if performed attentively and ceaselessly for a long period of time." *Sūtra* 1.14, Raveh, *Exploring the Yogasūtra*, p. 128.
2. J. Mascaro, trans., *The Bhagavad Gita*, revised edition (Delhi: Penguin Classics, 2009), p. 73.
3. R. Maharshi, *Eternal Consciousness: Conversation with Ramana Maharshi 1935–1939*, trans. Lily Benatav (Tel Aviv: Gal, 1994), p. 29 (in Hebrew).
4. *Sūtra* 3, Raveh, *Exploring the Yogasūtra*, p. 134.
5. Mehta, *Yoga: The Art of Integration*, pp. 317–318.
6. J. Kornfield, *After the Ecstasy, The Laundry: How the Heart Grows Wise on the Spiritual Path* (New York: Bantam, 2001), pp. 158–159.
7. C. G. Jung, *Collected Works of C. G. Jung*, vol. 11: *Psychology and Religion: West and East* (Princeton, NJ: Princeton University Press, 1938), p. 131.
8. Retrieved from https://tricycle.org/trikedaily/rigpa-abuse.
9. G. Feuerstein, *Holy Madness: The Shock Tactics and Radical Teachings of Crazy-Wise Adepts, Holy Fools and Rascal Gurus* (New York: Penguin Books, 1992), p. 243.
10. Retrieved from www.verywellmind.com/psychology-schools-of-thought-2795247.
11. Retrieved from www.nature.com/articles/nature14659.
12. S. Finger, *Minds Behind the Brain: A History of the Pioneers and Their Discoveries* (New York: Oxford, 2000), pp. 22.
13. B. Kolb and I. Q. Whishaw, *Fundamentals of Human Neuropsychology* (San Francisco, CA: W. H. Freeman, 1980).
14. R. M. Ruff, "A Friendly Critique of Neuropsychology: Facing the Challenges of Our Future," *Archives of Clinical Neuropsychology*, vol. 18 (2003), pp. 847–864.

15. M. R. Gerber and E. B. Gerber, "An Introduction to Trauma and Health," in M. Gerber, ed., *Trauma-Informed Healthcare Approaches* (Cham: Springer, 2019).
16. Retrieved from www.psychologytoday.com/us/blog/stress-relief/201709/trauma-informed-approaches-the-good-and-the-bad.
17. H. Coward, *Yoga and Psychology: Language, Memory, and Mysticism* (Albany, NY: State University of New York Press, 2002), p. 92.
18. G. Feuerstein, *The Psychology of Yoga: Integrating Eastern and Western Approaches for Understanding the Mind* (Boston, MA: Shambhala, 2014).
19. Ibid., p. xi.
20. Ibid., pp. 5, 19.
21. Retrieved from www.verywellmind.com/psychology-schools-of-thought-2795247
22. "He is the guru of even the yogin-s of the past, being unbound by time." *Sūtra* 1.26, Raveh, *Exploring the Yogasūtra*, p. 128; and "As a result of devotion to īśvara, samādhi is attained." *Sūtra* 1.45, ibid., p. 132.
23. Raveh, *Philosophical Threads in Patañjali's Yoga*, p. 124.
24. Object-oriented meditation requires uniformity and continuity of concentration at the same time. The practitioner concentrates continuously on an object, steadfastly and uniformly in which the object alone occupies and "colors" the mind. This is an object-oriented meditation composed of three limbs of yoga meditation: the *dhāraṇā*, the *dhyāna* and the *samādhi*.
25. Āraṇya, *Yoga Philosophy of Patañjali*, p. 255.
26. Eye movement, a principal component of EMDR, is reminiscent of eye movement exercises practiced in certain schools of yoga, such as that of Swami Shivananda or Sri Aurobindo. In these yoga exercises, eye movements improve concentration, vision and eye health, and help achieve a calm state of mind.
27. F. Shapiro and M. S. Forrest, *EMDR: The Breakthrough Therapy for Overcoming Anxiety, Stress, and Trauma* (New York: Basic Books, 1997), pp. 9–10.
28. R. Miller, "The Feeling-State Theory of Impulse-Control Disorders and the Impulse-Control Disorder Protocol," *Traumatology*, vol. 16, no. 2 (2010), pp. 2–10.
29. Ibid., pp. 3–4.
30. Ibid., p. 4.
31. Miller, "The Feeling-State Theory," p. 6.

Chapter 5

1. Ifergan, *The Man from Samye*, pp. 57–58.
2. See *sūtra* 2.29, Bryant, *The Yoga Sūtras of Patañjali*.
3. Dalai Lama, *Mind in Comfort and Ease: The Vision of Enlightenment in the Great Perfection* (Somerville, MA: Wisdom Publications, 2007), p. 80.
4. Nubchen Yeshe in C. J. Ying, "Being and Knowing in Wholeness, Chinese Chan, Tibetan Dzogchen, and the Logic of Immediacy in Contemplation," PhD thesis, Rice University, Houston, TX, p. 284.
5. *Sūtra* 2.46, Raveh, *Exploring the Yogasūtra*, p. 132.
6. Nubchen Yeshe in Ying, "Being and Knowing in Wholeness," p. 285.
7. "The conjunction between the seer and that which is seen is the cause [of suffering] to be avoided." *Sūtra* 2.17, Bryant, *The Yoga Sūtras of Patañjali*, p. 213.
8. "The means to liberation is uninterrupted discriminative discernment." *Sūtra* 2.26, Bryant, *The Yoga Sūtras of Patañjali*, p. 234.
9. For Longchenpa's extended biography and discussion about his works, see also Ifergan, *The Man from Samye*, pp. 53–72.
10. Ibid., pp. 5–9.
11. H. V. Guenther, "Preface," in Longchenpa, *Kindly Bent to Ease Us, Part 1: Mind*, trans. and annotated by H. V. Guenther (Berkeley, CA: Dharma Publishing, 1975), p. xxiv.
12. S. Van Schaik, *Approaching the Great Perfection: Simultaneous and Gradual Methods of Dzogchen Practice in the Longchen Nyingtig* (Boston, MA: Wisdom Publications, 2004), pp. 57, 59.
13. D. Higgins, "The Philosophical Foundations of Classical RDzogs Chen In Tibet: Investigating the Distinction between Dualistic Mind (sems) and Primordial Knowing (ye Shes)," *Wiener Studien zur Tibetologie und Buddhismuskunde*, no. 78 (2013), p. 57.

Chapter 6

1. Van Schaik, *Approaching the Great Perfection.*
2. When Longchenpa listed the twelve phases of dependent origination of conditional formation (the Buddhist theory referring to the emergence of the false perception or the partial and relative knowledge, *avidyā*), he also included the term Tibetan du-je (identical to the term *saṃskāra* in Sanskrit). This term represents only mental imprint, as opposed to *bag chags* (identical to the term *vāsanā* in Sanskrit), which also represents a

pattern of action and character. Although these two Tibetan concepts are similar to Patañjali's Sanskrit concepts, Longchenpa used the term *bag chags* to point to both the mental imprints as well as the patterns of behavior and character traits. Van Schaik, *Approaching the Great Perfection*, p. 59.

3. Longchenpa, *A Treasure Trove of Scriptural Transmission: A Commentary on the Precious Basic Space of Phenomena*, trans. T. R. Chagdud and R. Barron (Junction City, CA: Padma Publications, 2001), p. 279.
4. F. D. Germano and S. W. Waldron, "A Comparison of Alaya-Vijñana in Yogācāra and Dzogchen," in D. K Nauriyal, M. S. Drummond and Y. B. Lal, eds., *Buddhist Thought and Applied Psychological Research: Transcending the Boundaries* (New York: Routledge, 2006), p. 62.
5. According to the oral instructions of *The Six Yogas of Naropa* by Tsong-kha-pa, the body is regarded as being composed of a collection of coarse/physical and subtle/metaphysiological channels or nerves that are to be brought under control by means of yogic physical postures, breathing exercises, visualization, and so on. See G. H. Mullin, trans., *The Six Yogas of Naropa* (Boston, MA: Snow Lion Press, 2006), p. 27. Of the subtle, metaphysiological channels, there are three main systems; two are located to the sides of the central channel, termed *avadhūti* (located in proximity to the spine). When performing a specific breathing exercise, the air inhaled through the nostrils connects with the two channels that are to the sides of the *avadhūti*, and the vital energy generated with the breathing is forced into the middle channel (which is parallel to the spine), rising upward and igniting the heat in the region of navel that initiates an experience of bliss unified with clarity.
6. Longchenpa, *A Treasure Trove*, p. 279.
7. Ibid.
8. Longchenpa, *La Liberté Naturelle de L'esprit*, trans. and ed. P. Cornu (Paris: Editions du Seuil, 1994), p. 272.
9. Ibid. "Visit places that generate blessed, frightening or painful births, at the top of a mountain, in a cemetery, or in an abandoned valley ..."
10. J. William, *The Varieties of Religious Experience: A study in Human nature*, trans. Ya'akov Kopilevitch (Jerusalem: Bialik Institute, 1902), p. 140 (in Hebrew).
11. B. Guinagh, *Catharsis and Cognition in Psychotherapy* (New York: Springer, 1987), p. 14.
12. Ibid., p. v.

13. Longchenpa, *A Treasure Trove*, p. 290.
14. Ibid., p. 292.
15. Ibid., pp. 292–293.
16. "Ultimate *vairāgya* is thirstlessness toward the *guṇas*, arising from the vision of *puruṣa* (puruṣa-khyāti)." *Sūtra* 1.16, Raveh, *Exploring the Yogasūtra*, p. 127.
17. P. Fenner, "Buddha at the Gas Pump Interview," retrieved from www.youtube.com/watch?v=J3OAt0XQuYU.
18. See also E. Dacher, "Natural Awareness—The Wish-Fulfilling Gem: Notes from a Fellow Traveller," 2009, retrieved from http://elliottdacher.typepad.com. Dacher repeats the word "time" about thirty times in many compound forms such as "length of time," "over time," "maturation over time" to indicate that this is a lengthy process.
19. Kornfield does not mention the school in Tibetan Buddhism the two lamas belong, so it is impossible to know whether they belong to the tradition of Dzogchen. Thus, it is impossible to learn from these testimonies that the practice of Dzogchen is ineffective in dismantling mental imprints, tendencies, and patterns of behavior in the short term. But these testimonies emerge from the Tibetan-Buddhist way of life, and they deal with states of consciousness and other situations that are not foreign to Dzogchen.
20. Kornfield, *After the Ecstasy, The Laundry*, p. 155.
21. Ibid., pp. 206–207.
22. Welwood, "Embodying Your Realization," pp. 1–2.
23. G. Nixon, "Diving into the Fire of Trauma: A Nondual Approach to Healing and Awakening," *Journal of Nondual Psychology*, vol. 5 (2013), p. 3.
24. J. Prendergast, P. Fenner and S. Krystal, eds., *Sacred Mirror: Nondual Wisdom and Psychotherapy* (Saint Paul, MN: Omega Books, 2003), pp. 2–4.
25. Nixon, "Diving into the Fire of Trauma," p. 9.
26. Ibid., pp. 9–10.
27. Ibid., pp. 10–11.
28. Prendergast et al., *Sacred Mirror*, pp. 3–4.
29. Longchenpa, *A Treasure Trove*, p. 291.
30. Krystal in Prendergast et al., *Sacred Mirror*, p. 117. Interestingly, in the discussion of the integrated treatment of non-duality and Western psychological methods, Krystal also chose EMDR, a method I presented in the previous chapter, based on Miller's article and the case study he presented there. See Prendergast et al., ibid., pp. 120–135.

31. In Tibetan, "*ngo sprod*."
32. Ifergan, *The Man from Samye*, p. 131.

Epilogue

1. See *sūtras* 2.35–2.45, Raveh, *Exploring the Yogasūtra*, p. 132.
2. *Sūtra* 2.31, Raveh, *Exploring the Yogasūtra*, p. 132: "Observing these [*yamas*], irrespective of birth, place, time circumstances, or even a sense of duty, is 'the great vow' [mahāvrata]."

Glossary

1. S. van Schaik, "Early Dzogchen IV: The Role of Atiyoga," 2011, retrieved from https://earlytibet.com/2011/08/03/early-dzogchen-iv.
2. Nubchen Yeshe in S. G. Karmay Karmay, *The Great Perfection: A Philosophical and Meditative Teaching of Tibetan Buddhism* (Leiden: Brill, 2007), p. 107.

Bibliography

Āraṇya, H. *Yoga Philosophy of Patañjali: Containing his Yoga Aphorisms with Vyasa's Commentary in Original Sanskrit and Annotations Thereon with Copious Hints on the Practice of Yoga*. Calcutta: Calcutta University Press, 1981.

Arya, U. *Yoga-sūtras of Patañjali with the Exposition of Vyasa: A Translation and Commentary, Volume I—Samādhi-pāda*. Honesdale, PA: Himalayan Institute Press, 1986.

Azar, B. "A New Take on Psychoneuroimmunology." *Monitor on Psychology*, 32(11) (2001): 34–36.

Berke, J. H. "Shame and Envy." *British Journal of Psychotherapy*, 2(4) (1986): 262–270.

Bloom, P. *Against Empathy: The Case for Rational Compassion*. London: Bodley Head, 2016.

Booth, P. "Emotional Disclosure and Psychoneuroimmunology." In K. Vedhara and M. Irwin, eds., *Human Psychoneuroimmunology*. Oxford: Oxford University Press, 2005.

Bryant, E. F. *The Yoga Sūtras of Patañjali: A New Edition, Translation and Commentary*. New York: North Point Press, 2009.

Chapple, C. K. and A. L. Funes Maderey (eds.). *Thinking with the Yoga Sūtra of Patañjali: Translation and Interpretation*. London: Lexington Books, 2019.

Clarke, J. H. "The Metapsychology of Character Change: A Case Study of Ebenezer Scrooge." *Journal of Spirituality in Mental Health*, 11(4) (2009): 248–263.

Columba, S. "The Desert Fathers on Radical Self-Honesty." *Vox Benedictina*, 8(1) (1991): 7–54.

Coward, H. *Yoga and Psychology: Language, Memory, and Mysticism*. Albany, NY: State University of New York Press, 2002.

Csaba, K. "The Matsyendrasaṃhitā: A Yoginī-Centered 13th-Century Yoga Text of the South Indian *Śāmbhava* Cult." In D. Lorenzen and A. Muñoz, eds., *Yogi Heroes and Poets: Histories and legends of the Nāths*. Albany, NY: SUNY Press, 2011.

Dalai Lama. *Mind in Comfort and Ease: The Vision of Enlightenment in the Great Perfection*. Somerville, MA: Wisdom Publications, 2007.

Dickens, C. *A Christmas Carol and Other Christmas Writings*. London: Penguin 2003 [1843].

Eliot, T. S. *Four Quartets*. London: Faber & Faber, 2001 [1941].

Engler, J. "Promises and Perils of the Spiritual Path." In M. Unno, ed., *Buddhism and Psychotherapy Across Cultures*. Boston, MA: Wisdom Publications, 2006.

Feuerstein, G. *Encyclopedic Dictionary of Yoga*. Saint Paul, MN: Paragon House,1990.

Feuerstein, G. *Holy Madness: The Shock Tactics and Radical Teachings of Crazy-Wise Adepts, Holy Fools and Rascal Gurus*. New York: Penguin Books, 1992.

Feuerstein, G. *The Philosophy of Classical Yoga*. Rochester, VT: Inner Traditions, 1996.

Feuerstein, G. *The Psychology of Yoga: Integrating Eastern and Western Approaches for Understanding the Mind*. Boston, MA: Shambhala, 2014.

Feuerstein, G. *The Yoga-Sūtra of Patañjali: A New Translation and Commentary*. Rochester, VT: Inner Traditions, 1989.

Finger, S. *Minds Behind the Brain: A History of the Pioneers and Their Discoveries*. New York: Oxford, 2000.

Gerber, M. R. and E. B. Gerber. "An Introduction to Trauma and Health." In M. Gerber, ed., *Trauma-Informed Healthcare Approaches*. Cham: Springer, 2019.

Germano, F. D. and S. W. Waldron. "A Comparison of Alaya-Vijñana in Yogācāra and Dzogchen." In D. K Nauriyal, M. S. Drummond and Y. B. Lal, eds., *Buddhist Thought and Applied Psychological Research: Transcending the Boundaries*. New York: Routledge, 2006.

Grinshpon, Y. *Silence and Liberation in Classical Yoga*. Tel Aviv: Ministry of Defense, Israel, 2002.

Grinshpon, Y. *Silence Unheard: Deathly Otherness in Pātañjala-Yoga*. Albany, NY: State University of New York Press, 2001.

Guenther, H. V. "Preface." In Longchenpa, *Kindly Bent to Ease Us, Part 1: Mind*, trans. and annotated by H. V. Guenther. Berkeley, CA: Dharma Publishing, 1975.

Guinagh, B. *Catharsis and Cognition in Psychotherapy*. New York: Springer, 1987.

Halbfass, W. *Tradition and Reflection: Explorations in Indian Thought*. New York: State University of New York Press, 1991.

Harrison, M. C. "The Paradox of Fiction and the Ethics of Empathy: Reconceiving Dickens's Realism." *Narrative*, 16(3) (2008): 256–278.

Henshaw, S. "Why Positive Affirmations Don't Work." *Psych Central*, 2015, https://psychcentral.com.

Higgins, D. "The Philosophical Foundations of Classical RDzogs Chen In Tibet: Investigating the Distinction between Dualistic Mind (sems) and Primordial Knowing (ye Shes)." *Wiener Studien zur Tibetologie und Buddhismuskunde*, 78 (2013).

Horney, K. *Our Inner Conflicts: A Constructive Theory of Neurosis*. New York: W. W. Norton, 1992 [1945].

Ifergan, G. *The Man from Samye: Longchenpa on Praxis, Its Negation and Liberation*. New Delhi: Aditya Prakashan, Aditya Prakashan, 2014.

Jakubczak, M. "The Sense of Ego-maker in Classical Sāṃkhya and Yoga: Reconsideration of Ahaṃkāra." *Cracow Indological Studies*, 10 (2008).

Jung, C. G. *Collected Works of C. G. Jung, vol. 11: Psychology and Religion: West and East*. Princeton, NJ: Princeton University Press, 1938.

Karmay Karmay, S. G. *The Great Perfection: A Philosophical and Meditative Teaching of Tibetan Buddhism*. Leiden: Brill, 2007.

Klein, M. *Envy and Gratitude, and Other Works, 1946–1963*. New York: Free Press, 1984.

Kolb, B. and I. Q. Whishaw. *Fundamentals of Human Neuropsychology*. San Francisco, CA: W. H. Freeman, 1980.

Kornfield, J. *After the Ecstasy, The Laundry: How the Heart Grows Wise on the Spiritual Path*. New York: Bantam, 2001.

Krishnamurti, J. *Freedom from the Known*. San Francisco, CA: Harper, 2009.

Longchenpa. *A Treasure Trove of Scriptural Transmission: A Commentary on the Precious Basic Space of Phenomena*, trans. T. R. Chagdud and R. Barron. Junction City, CA: Padma Publications, 2001.

Longchenpa. *La Liberté Naturelle de L'esprit*, trans. and ed. P. Cornu. Paris: Editions du Seuil, 1994.

Maharshi, R. *Eternal Consciousness: Conversation with Ramana Maharshi 1935–1939*, translated by Lily Benatav. Tel Aviv: Gal, 1994.

Mascaro, J., trans. *The Bhagavad Gita*, revised edition. Delhi: Penguin Classics, 2009.

Mehta, R. *Yoga: The Art of Integration: A Commentary on the Yoga Sūtras of Patañjali*. India: The Theosophical Publishing House, 1990.

Miller, R. "The Feeling-State Theory of Impulse-Control Disorders and the Impulse-Control Disorder Protocol." *Traumatology*, 16(2) (2010): 2–10.

Miller, A. *The Drama of the Gifted Child: The Search for the True Self*. Tel Aviv: Dvir, 1992.

Mishra, N. "Saṃskāras in Yoga Philosophy and Western Psychology." *Philosophy East and West*, 2(4) (1953): 308–316.

Mishra, R. S. *The Textbook of Yoga Psychology: The Definitive Translation and Interpretation of Patañjali's Yoga Sūtras*. New York: Baba Bhagavandas Publication Trust, 1997.

Mullin, G. H., trans. *The Six Yogas of Naropa*. Boston, MA: Snow Lion Press, 2006.

Nixon, G. "Diving into the Fire of Trauma: A Nondual Approach to Healing and Awakening." *Journal of Nondual Psychology*, 5 (2013).

Norbu, N. *Dream Yoga and the Practice of Natural Light*. New York: Snow Lion, 2002.

Norbu, N. *The Cycle of Day and Night*, trans. J. Reynolds. Barrytown, NY: Station Hill Press, 2000.

Olivelle, P., trans. *The Early Upaniṣads*. Delhi: Oxford University Press, 1998.

Prendergast, J., P. Fenner and S. Krystal, eds. *Sacred Mirror: Nondual Wisdom and Psychotherapy*. Saint Paul, MN: Omega Books, 2003.

Proeve, M. and S. Tudor. *Remorse: Psychological and Jurisprudential Perspectives*. Abingdon: Routledge, 2010.

Raveh, D. *Exploring the Yogasūtra: Philosophy and Translation*, annotated edition. London: Continuum, 2012.

Raveh, D. *Philosophical Threads in Patañjali's Yoga*. Tel Aviv: Hakibutz Hameuchad, 2010.

Ruff, R. M. "A Friendly Critique of Neuropsychology: Facing the Challenges of Our Future." *Archives of Clinical Neuropsychology*, 18 (2003).

Rukmani, T. S., trans. and ed. *Yogavārttika of Vijñānabhikṣu: Samādhipāda*, vol. 2. Delhi: Munshiram Manoharlal Publishers, 2007.

Shapiro, F. and M. S. Forrest. *EMDR: The Breakthrough Therapy for Overcoming Anxiety, Stress, and Trauma*. New York: Basic Books, 1997.

Shulman, D. *More than Real: A History of the Imagination in South India*. Cambridge, MA: Harvard University Press, 2012.

Tola, F. and C. Dragonetti. *The Yogasūtras of Patañjali on Concentration of Mind*, trans. K. D. Prithipaul. India: Motilal Banarsidass, 1955.

Trungpa, C. *Cutting Through Spiritual Materialism*. Boston, MA: Shambhala, 1987.

Van Schaik, S. *Approaching the Great Perfection: Simultaneous and Gradual Methods of Dzogchen Practice in the Longchen Nyingtig*. Boston, MA: Wisdom Publications, 2004.

Welwood, J. *Toward a Psychology of Awakening: Buddhism, Psychotherapy, and the Path of Personal and Spiritual Transformation*. Boston, MA: Shambhala, 2000.

Wenzlaff, R. M. W. and D. M. Wegner. "Thought Suppression." *Annual Review of Psychology*, 51 (2000): 59–91.

Werner, K. "Yoga and the Ṛg Veda: An Interpretation of the Keśin Hymn." *Religious Studies*, 13(3) (September 1977): 289–302.

Whicher, I. "Cessation and Integration in Classical Yoga." *Asian Philosophy*, 5(1) (1995): 47–58.

Whicher, I. "The Liberating Role of Saṃskāra in Classical Yoga." *Journal of Indian Philosophy*, 33(5) (2005): 601–630.

White, D. G. *The Yoga Sūtra of Patañjali: A Biography*. Princeton, NJ: Princeton University Press, 2014.

William, J. *The Varieties of Religious Experience: A Study in Human Nature*, trans. Ya'akov Kopilevitch. Jerusalem: Bialik Institute, 1902.

Williams, M. *A Sanskrit-English Dictionary Etymologically and Philologically Arranged with Special Reference to Cognate Indo-European Languages*. Varanasi: Indica, 1996.

Wood, J., W. E. Perunovic and J. Lee. "Positive Self-Statements: Power for Some, Peril for Others." *Psychological Science*, 20(7) (2009): 860–866.

Ying, C. J. "Being and Knowing in Wholeness, Chinese Chan, Tibetan Dzogchen, and the Logic of Immediacy in Contemplation." PhD thesis, Rice University, Houston, TX.

Index

Note: page numbers followed by *n* refer to notes.

Bloom, Paul 62
breathing/breath control
  Dzogchen 121, 164*n*5
  prāṇāyāma 3, 11, 111, 151, 155*n*11, 156*n*12
Bṛhadāraṇyaka Upaniṣad 37, 78
Bryant, Edwin Francis 13, 57–58, 65–66, 142
Buddha nature 112
buddhi 10, 19, 22, 77, 148
Buddhism 1, 9–10, 16, 32, 109, 117
  four truths of 8
  and six modes of existence 126–127
  Tibetan *see* Dzogchen
Burley, Mike 14

catharsis 128–129, 144, 145
Chakrabarti, Arindam 14
chakras 121
Chapple, Christopher 14
child abuse 2, 55–56, 135
children/childhood 20–21, 39, 40
Christianity 60–61
Christmas Carol, A (Dickens) 38–40, 76–77, 79–80
citta 11, 19–20, 148
cognition 19–20, 27
cognitive psychology 95, 97, 98–99, 129
cognitive-behavioral therapy 107
compassion 1, 2, 5, 43, 51, 55, 67, 76, 80, 89, 98, 107
compulsive disorders 7, 102–108, 145
  and Dzogchen 113, 137
  and feeling state 103–104, 105, 106, 107
  and negative/positive beliefs 104, 106
  and yoga 107–108
concentration (*samādhi*) 11, 12–13, 26, 41, 111, 152, 162*n*24
conceptualization (*vikalpa*) 19
Corigliano, Stephanie 14
courage 65, 66–67, 69, 85, 136
Coward, Harold 96–97
craving *see* desire/craving
crazy wisdom 91–93
cultivating the opposite *see* *pratipakṣa bhāvanā*

Dacher, Elliott 131–132
Dalai Lama 112
darkness *see tamas*
death 25
  fear of (*abhinivesha*) 28, 34–36, 38, 40
defense mechanisms 27, 35, 52, 60, 65, 84, 89, 90, 91, 99, 102
deity, visualization of 71–72, 74
denial 6, 35
depression 2, 5, 6, 129–130, 137
desire/craving 4, 5, 8, 9, 10, 14, 32–34, 54
  and memory 23
  see also greed
dhāraṇa 111, 148
Dharma 1, 98–99
dharmakāya 118, 138–139, 148–149
dhyāna 45–46, 50, 73, 111, 149, 162*n*24
Dickens, Charles 38–40, 76–77, 79–80
direct perception (*pratyakṣa*) 19, 34, 73, 88–89, 92
dispassion (*vairāgya*) *see* awareness, uninvolved
dreams 20–23, 36
  and ignorance (*avidyā*) 21, 28–29
  as omens 22–23

dualism 13, 110, 111, 116, 122, 123
duḥkha 8, 9, 14, 58, 75, 87, 149
dveṣa 28, 32–34, 38, 40, 83–84, 106
Dyson, Damcho 92
Dzogchen 16–17, 108, 109–120, 149
  and "crazy wisdom" 91–92
  and engaging the mind 113, 114–115
  as immediate/effortless 16, 110, 112–113, 119–120
  and Indian yoga, compared 109, 110–120
  and *A Lamp for the Eye in Contemplation* 110, 113–115
  and Longchenpa *see* Longchenpa
  and non-action 16, 112, 113, 114, 115
  and non-duality 17, 110, 118, 119, 124
  and Padmasambhava 109–110
  physical methods of 113–114
  and sleep/dreams 21, 22–23
Dzogchen, psychology of 109, 120, 121–140
  and aspects of mind 121–123
  and cathartic practice 125–131, 144
  and choiceless awareness 134–135, 136, 139, 140
  and conscious/unconscious 122
  and *dharmakāya* 118, 138–139, 148–149
  and direct introduction 139–140
  and duality 122–123
  and habitual tendencies *see bag chags*
  and mental imprints 121, 122, 123, 124, 125–126, 127, 128, 129, 132–133
  and natural awareness 112, 118, 122, 123, 124, 128, 131, 134–140
  and natural release method 130, 131–132
  and practitioners' testimonies 132–134, 165*n*19
  and self-liberation 125, 126, 128, 131
  and six modes of existence 126–127
  and therapists of non-duality 136–138

ego 12, 24, 33, 48, 77
  and *avidyā* 28
  and crazy wisdom yogis 91–92, 93
  illusion of permanence of 8
  role of 31
  see also asmitā
Eliot, T. S. 5
embarrassment 63, 64, 84
EMDR (eye movement desensitization and reprocessing) 102–103, 134, 165*n*30
  and anxiety 102, 103
  and cognitive-behavioral therapy, compared 107
  and gambling addiction 105–107
  and yoga 107, 162*n*26
emotional crisis 1, 2, 89–90, 90, 107
emotions 3, 23, 33, 40, 59–60, 73
  avoiding/suppressing 7, 8, 53–55, 63
  and compulsive disorders 103–104
  desire to transcend 5–6
  and Dzogchen 124, 125–131
  and memory (*smṛti*) 23, 26–27

and psychology 100
and Self 7–8
and self-honesty 59–61
sharing/expressing 65, 67
see also specific emotions
empathy 51, 61–62, 69, 72, 80, 82
emptiness 31, 32, 89, 135
Engler, Jack 2
envy 76, 129, 137
epistemology 12, 97, 117, 121, 123
eye movements *see* EMDR

father 55–56
fear 20, 26, 85
of anger 55, 56, 67, 69
of death (*abhinivesha*) 28, 34–36, 38, 40
and identity 31–32
feeling states 103–104, 105, 106, 107
Fenner, Peter 131
Feuerstein, Georg 13, 15, 142, 157*n*17
on crazy wisdom 92–93
on cultivating the opposite 56–57
on *saṃskāras* 41, 42–43, 58, 65
on yoga and psychology 96, 97–98
Freud, Sigmund 31, 96, 97, 159*n*22
Funes Maderey, Ana Laura 14

gambling addiction 103, 104–107, 145
and EMDR 105–107
Gandhi, Mahātmā 15
generosity 75, 80
gestalt psychology 95, 97
gods
dimensions of 126–127
encounters with 4
greed 14, 39, 40, 58, 61, 75–77, 79–80
Grinshpon, Yohanan 13, 24, 41, 78
Guenther, Herbert 117–118
guilt 63, 64, 94
Guinagh, Barry 128–129
guṇas 21–22, 47, 149, 155*n*7
guru-teachers 100–101

habitual tendencies (*bag chags*) 121, 123–124, 125, 127, 130, 148, 163–164*n*2
habitual tendencies (*vāsanās*) 38–40, 56, 75, 80, 96, 102, 120
Harrison, Mary-Catherine 76
healing 8, 9–10, 99, 101
and cultivating the opposite 14, 34, 84–86
and therapy 84–86, 106–107, 135–136, 138
Hick, John 97
Higgins, David 118
Hinduism 16, 22, 109
horror 32
humanistic psychology 95, 97–98

identifications 3, 8, 9, 10, 21, 35, 38
see also avidyā; ego
identity 23, 27, 40, 48
fear of loss of 31–32
ignorance (*ajñāna*) 14, 58, 59, 75, 87
ignorance (*avidyā*) 21, 28–29, 44, 51, 66, 100, 120, 142, 143, 147, 163*n*2
il y a 32
imagining (*bhāvanā*) 15, 71–73
impulsive disorders 102, 103
inferential knowledge (*anumāna*) 19
insight meditation 57, 58, 65–66
insight (*vivekakhyāti*) 11, 12, 13, 26, 35
intellect (*buddhi*) 10, 19, 22, 73, 77
Īśvara praṇidhāna 73

Jainism 16, 109
jealousy 5, 7, 23, 76, 129–130
joy 28, 33, 55, 84
judgement 14, 19
Jung, Carl 96, 97

kaivalya 149
karma 27, 28, 37, 63, 67, 75, 96, 113, 123, 124, 137, 149
Keśin yogi 4, 5, 7, 8–9, 10, 11, 17, 26, 36, 44, 66, 141, 149
Kevala-Kumbhaka 11, 150
Kiss, Csaba 72
Klein, Melanie 76
kleśas 27–36, 73, 74, 150
  and *abhinivesha* 28, 34–36
  and *asmitā* 19, 28, 29–32
  and *avidyā* 21, 28–29, 44
  cultivating the opposite of *see* opposite, cultivating
  dormant/weakened/suspended/active 36
  and *klișța/aklișța* 42–43
  and mixed feelings 34
  and pairs of opposites 32–33, 83–85, 86
  and *pratiprasava* 47
  and psychology 96, 102
  and *rāga/dveșa* 28, 32–34, 35, 40
  and *saṃskāras* 38, 40, 42–43
  and two foundations of practice (*abhyāsa/vairāgya*) 69
  and *vāsanās* 38, 39, 96, 102
klișța 42–43
knowledge, correct/valid (*pramāṇa*) 19
knowledge, false (*viparyaya*) 19
knowledge, inferential (*anumāna*) 19, 34

Kolb, B. 96
Kornfield, Jack 89–90, 93, 107, 132, 165*n*19
Krishna, Daya 25
Krishnamurti, Jiddu 25, 134
Krystal, Sheila 138, 165*n*30
kumbhaka 11
kuṇḍalinī 72

labeling 14, 19, 123, 130, 131, 138
Lama Zhang 115
Lamp for the Eye in Contemplation, A (Nubchen Yeshe) 110, 113–115
Levinas, Emmanuel 32
Lhatong 150
liberation 1, 5, 8, 15, 24–25, 46, 49, 110–111, 143
  and Dzogchen 17, 109, 110, 113
  and ego 31
  and insight/wisdom 9, 155*n*10
  and separation/return 25
loneliness 6, 39, 40
Longchenpa 16, 108, 115, 116–118, 120
  and mental imprints 125–126
  and natural awareness 139
  and non-duality 137
  and practice of acting out emotions 125–131, 144
  and psychology, compared 129
  and *samsara* 123
  and self-liberation 125, 126, 128, 131
love 1, 4, 5, 7, 34, 79, 98

mahā-vratam 17, 150
Maharshi, Ramana 87
Maitreyī 78
manas 19, 150

mārga 8
Maslow, Abraham 97–98
Matsyendrasahitā 72
mauna 4, 24, 27, 88, 89, 107, 147*n*16, 157*n*16
meditation (*bhāvanā*) 1, 3, 15, 16, 42, 71
  and cultivating the opposite *see pratipakṣa bhāvana*
  and *dhyāna* 45–46, 50, 73, 111, 149, 162*n*24
  and dreams 21, 156*n*4
  Dzogchen 113–114, 124, 131–132, 140
  insight 57, 58, 65–66
  mindfulness (*Satipatthana*) 58, 98–99
  as non-judgemental reflection 49
  object-oriented 43, 111, 140, 162*n*24
  repetitive (*abhyāsa*) 68, 69, 78, 87
  and *samādhi* 11, 12–13, 26, 41, 111, 162*n*24
  Samyama 101, 152
  and transformation 2
Mehta, Rohit 13, 15, 49, 57, 58, 65, 88–89
memory (*smṛti*) 8, 19–20, 23–27, 33
  and emotions 23, 26–27
  as fluctuation (*vṛitti*)) 23
  and forgetfulness 25
  Krishnamurti on 25–26
  and liberation 24–25
  loss of 23–24
  and psychology 95, 96, 102–103, 107
  suppression of 54, 55
mental imprints (*saṃskāras*) 6, 7, 8, 20–21, 27, 29, 35, 37–44, 120, 152, 155*n*7
  and addiction 105–106
  blocking/pacifying 15–16
  contradictory forces of 45
  and cultivating the opposite *see pratipakṣa bhāvana*
  direct perception of 19, 34, 73, 88–89
  and Dzogchen 121, 163–164*n*2
  and habitual tendencies *see vāsanās*
  and imagining the opposite 75
  and karma 37
  and *kleśas* 38, 40, 42–43
  nirodha 8, 24, 40–42, 88
  and *pratiprasava* 48
  and repetition of affirmations 52
  and stillness of mind 42
  and therapy 95, 145
  vyutthāna/nirodha 40–42
mental processes 19–20, 27, 47, 53
mental stillness 4, 5, 13, 16, 21, 24, 42, 46, 50, 51, 57–58, 68, 78, 100, 107
  and Lhatong 150
metaphysics 13, 121, 156*n*7
Miller, Robert 103, 104–105, 134, 145, 165*n*30
mind
  and discerning insight *see* insight
  and Dzogchen 114–115, 121–123
  healthy 7
  intelligence of (reason/*buddhi*) 10, 19, 22, 77
  and *kleśas see kleśas*
  and mirror metaphor 11–12

and psychology 95
and true Self 10, 12, 13
see also citta
mindfulness meditation (*Satipatthana*) 58, 98–99
mirror metaphor 11–12, 13, 30
Mishra, Ramamurti 41, 53, 55, 56
Monier-Williams, Monier 71
moral codes 4–5, 14, 15, 17, 49, 51, 111
and psychology 108
see also yoga ethics
moral philosophy 17, 142

negative thoughts/behaviours 14, 15
neuropsychology 95–96, 97
New Age thinking 7, 31, 52
nidrā see sleep
nirodha saṃskāras 8, 24, 40–42, 88, 119, 150
nirvana 118, 150
Nixon, Gary 134–136, 138
niyama 111, 150
non-action 16, 112, 113, 114, 115
non-duality 17, 110, 118, 119, 124
therapists of 136–138, 140
non-judgement 134, 135
now 77–78
Nubchen Yeshe 110, 113–115
Nyingma school 150–151

Obama, Barack 62–63
obsessions 7, 113
see also compulsive disorders
obsessive-compulsive behavior *see* compulsive disorders
Om 77
omens (*ariṣṭa*) 22–23, 156*n*8
one-pointed concentration 41–42, 50, 140, 141, 143
opposite, imagining (*pratipakṣa bhāvana*) 14, 71–86
and cultivating the opposite, dual practice of 73–75, 80
exercise 80–83
and greed 75–77, 79–80
and images of possible future 74–75, 79–80, 82–83
and *kleśa*s as pairs of opposites 32–33, 83–86
origin/development of 71–73
and self-honesty 74, 75, 79, 81, 83
and visualization of the deity 71–72, 74
and vulnerable face of the other 81–82
opposite, psychological 87–94, 98, 100
and accomplished/"crazy wisdom" yogis 90–93
and deception of I-am-ness 93–94
and defense mechanisms 89, 90, 91, 99, 102
and direct perception 88–89
and emotional crisis 89–90
and shadow 90, 93
and time needed for practice 87, 89, 90, 94, 100, 144

Padmasambhava 109–110, 115
pain 1, 15–16, 26–27, 28–29, 54–55, 58–59, 84
avoidance of 5, 8, 33
and mental imprints 20, 21, 22, 23, 45
and remorse 63–64

passion (*rajas*) 10
Patañjali 3, 9
  see also Yoga Sūtras
patience 51, 52
perception (*pratyakṣa*) 19, 30, 34, 73, 88–89, 92
personality 3, 11
phenomenal world *see prakṛti*
Phillips, Stephen 14
pleasure 8, 10, 23, 25, 33
  and suffering 28, 84
poetry 71–72
posture
  and Dzogchen 113–114, 121
  emotional 51
  yogic (*āsana*) 68, 83, 85, 97, 111
prakṛti 21, 22, 29, 45, 47, 51
  and *guṇas* 21–22, 47, 155*n*7
  and memory 24, 25, 27
  and real Self, false connection between 9, 10, 11–12, 73, 116
pramāṇa 19
prāṇa 11
prāṇāyāma 3, 111, 151, 155*n*11, 156*n*12
pratipakṣa bhāvanā (cultivating the opposite) 7, 14–15, 17, 33, 45–69, 120, 142, 143
  and anger 51, 52, 54, 55–56, 65, 66–67, 69
  and controlling destructive impulses 53–55
  and *dhyāna* 45–46, 50
  as imagining the opposite *see* opposite, imagining
  and introspection 56–58
  and *pratiprasava see pratiprasava*
  and psychology 87–88, 98, 107, 143–144
  and reflection on consequences 58–69
  and remorse 59–60, 63–65, 66, 67, 69
  and repetition of affirmations 52–53
  and repetitive practice/dispassion (*abhyāsa/vairāgya*) 67–68, 69
  and self-honesty 59–61, 66, 67, 69, 143
  and sensitivity to others 59, 61–63, 66, 143
pratiprasava 45, 47–49, 51
  as intellectual method 49
  and involution 48
  psychological role of 47–48, 49
pratyāhāra 111, 151
pratyakṣa 19, 30, 34, 73, 88–89, 92
Prendergast, John 135, 136, 137, 138
Proeve, Michael 63
psychoanalysis 39, 95, 97
psychological dimensions of yoga 3, 13–14, 15, 87–108
  and cognitive psychology 95, 97, 98–99
  and cultivating the opposite 87–88, 98, 107, 143–145
  and Dzogchen *see* Dzogchen
  and eye movements *see* EMDR
  and gradual/immediate approaches 119–120
  and guru-teachers 100–101
  and humanistic psychology 95, 97–98
  and limits of human nature 96, 97
  and memory (*smṛti*) 19–20
  and neuropsychology 95–96
  and opposite 87–94
  and personal responsibility 101

and psychology/yoga compared 98–100, 107–108
and sleep (*nidrā*) 19–23
and transpersonal experience 96–97, 98
and trauma 95, 96, 107
psychology 16, 17, 94–101
as non-judgemental 108
opposite in *see* opposite, psychological
puruṣa see Self, real/pure

qualities *see guṇas*

rāga see attachment/attraction
rajas 22, 151
Raveh, Daniel 13, 25, 38, 101, 157*n*17, 158*nn*1, 6
reason (*buddhi*) 10, 19, 22, 77
reflection (*sattva*) 10
rejection (*dveṣa*) 28, 32–34, 38, 40, 83–84, 106
relationships 2, 4–5, 6, 7, 94, 101
remorse 15, 59–60, 63–65, 66, 67, 69, 74, 80
repetitive practice (*abhyāsa*) 68, 69, 78, 87, 114, 142, 147
responsibility 60, 63, 64, 81, 101, 143
rigpa 21, 110, 112, 113, 118, 151–152
Rigveda 4, 157*n*16
Rinchen, Gampopa Sonam 114
Rinpoche, Chögyal Namkhai Norbu 22–23
Rinpoche, Sogyal 92, 93
roga/roga-hetu 9
Ruff, R. M. 96
Rukmani, T. S. 13, 41

sākṣat-karaṇa 88–89
samādhi 11, 12–13, 26, 41, 111, 152, 162*n*24
Sāṅkhya 22, 152
samsara 77, 118, 123, 152
saṃskāras see mental imprints
samyama meditation 101, 152
Sāṅkhya system 72–73
Santana, Carlos 52, 56
Satipatthana 58, 98–99
sattva 10, 22, 153
Saundarya-lahari 72
Scrooge, Ebenezer 38–40, 76–77, 79–80
seed metaphor 47, 48
Self, real/pure (*puruṣa*) 9–13, 47, 66, 87, 111, 151
and breathing 11
and dreams 20
and *kleśas* 28, 29–30, 31, 32, 36
and *kundalini* 72
and memory 24, 27
and "now" 78–79
and phenomenal world 9, 10, 11–12, 24–25, 29, 73, 116
and selfhood, compared 99–100
and union/unification 12–13
self-awareness/sense of self 7, 28, 29–30, 39, 40, 58, 77, 78
self-esteem 6, 52, 53, 89, 107
self-honesty 5–6, 15, 59–61, 66, 67, 69
and imagining the opposite 74, 75, 79, 81, 83, 143
Self-knowledge 41, 72, 119
self-liberation 125, 126, 128, 131
Self-realization 5, 34, 35
self-release 128, 131, 140
self-transcendence 7

Selfhood 12, 13, 99
  Western concept of 99–100
sensitivity to others 15, 59, 61–63, 66, 76, 79, 83, 143
shame 6, 60, 61, 63–64, 84, 93, 106
Shapiro, Francine 102, 103
Sheinman, Nimrod 2
Shiva 71
Shulman, David 71, 72
siddhis see supernatural powers
silence (*mauna*) 4, 24, 27, 88, 89, 107, 157*n*16
sleep (*nidrā*) 19–23, 27
  dreamless 21–22
  see also dreams
smṛti see memory
sorrow 8, 11, 28, 63, 64, 77, 84, 127
Stewart, Columba 60–61
stinginess 38–40, 75
stress 54, 102, 145
suffering 6, 7, 24, 42, 45, 120, 155*n*7
  future, imagining 74–75
  and identification 3, 9, 11, 155*n*9
  and pleasure/joy 28
  and psychology 99, 100
  and sensitivity to others 59, 61–63
  see also duḥkha
supernatural powers (*siddhis*) 4, 11, 13, 89, 97, 100, 153

tamas 10, 153
  and amnesia 24
  and sleep/dreams 21–22
tantrism 17, 72, 73–74, 109, 142
testimony (*āgama*) 19, 34
Tibetan Buddhist yoga *see* Dzogchen
transcendental dimension of yoga 5, 7, 132
transpersonal psychology 96–97, 98
trauma 6, 23, 95, 96, 97, 107, 145
tṛṣṇa 8
Trungpa, Chögyam 31–32, 93
trust 2, 96, 101
Tudor, Steven 63

unconscious 122
Upaniṣads 37, 78, 153

Vācaspati, Miśra 13
vairāgya 17, 68, 69, 78, 87, 111, 131, 142, 143, 153
Vajrayāna 109, 153
vāsanās 38–40, 56, 75, 80, 96, 102, 120, 121, 153, 163*n*2
Vedas/Vedic culture 3–4, 153–154
Vijñānabhikṣu 11, 13, 15, 35, 78
vikalpa 19, 154
violence 14, 17, 55, 141
viparyaya 19
vipassanā meditation 2
Viveka-khyāti 11, 12, 13, 28, 154
Vivekānanda, Swami 13
vṛttis 23, 37, 154, 155*n*7
Vyāsa 9, 13, 15, 35, 36, 41–42, 101
  on cultivating the opposite 47–48, 51, 58–59, 61, 63, 64, 66, 68
  on violence 141–142
vyutthāna saṃskāras 40–42, 88, 119

Washburn, Michael 97
Wegner, D. M. 54, 55
Welwood, John 55, 56, 65, 67, 69, 133–134
Wenzlaff, R. M. W. 54, 55
Whicher, Ian 13, 25, 41
Whishaw, I. Q. 96

Wilber, Ken 97
wisdom, discerning (*Viveka-khyāti*) 11, 12, 13, 28, 29, 41, 73, 116
Wundt, Wilhelm 94–95

Yājñavalkya 78
yamas 14, 49, 58, 75, 87, 111, 154
yoga 1–3, 154
  benefits of 1
  commercialization of 7
  and cultivating the opposite *see* *pratipakṣa bhāvana*
  and emotions *see* emotions
  history/philosophy of 3
  and silence (*mauna*) 4, 24, 27, 88, 89, 107, 157*n*16
  and psychological conflict 1, 2, 6–7
  psychological dimensions of *see* psychological dimensions of yoga
  social aspects of 4–5
  three limbs of 162*n*24
  translations/commentaries of 13
  as union/unification 12–13
  and *yamas* 14, 49, 58, 75, 87, 111, 154
yoga ethics 15, 17, 59, 74, 82, 111, 141, 143, 150
Yoga Sūtras (Patañjali) 3, 4–5, 154
  and breathing *see* breathing/breath control
  commentaries/translations of 13, 14
  and concentrating on the opposite *see pratiprasava*
  and cultivating the opposite *see* *pratipakṣa bhāvanā*
  and Dzogchen, compared *see under* Dzogchen
  and eight limbs of yoga 46, 111
  and emotions 7–8, 58–59
  as gradual path 110–112, 119, 120
  and great vow 142–143, 150, 166*n*2
  and healing 8, 9–10, 14, 34, 99, 101
  and imagining the opposite *see* opposite, imagining
  and *kleśas see kleśas*
  and memory (*smṛti*) 23–24, 25, 26, 157*n*17
  and mental processes 19–20, 27
  "now" in 77–79
  and psychology/psychological opposite 87, 88–89, 100, 101
  and reward/punishment 141–142
  and *saṃskāras see* mental imprints
  and Sāṅkhya system 72–73
  and self-honesty *see* self-honesty
  and sleep/dreams 20–21, 22, 156*n*4
  and *yamas* 14

zhine 140, 150

www.ingramcontent.com/pod-product-compliance
Lightning Source LLC
Chambersburg PA
CBHW071846230426
43671CB00012B/2079
* 9 7 8 1 8 0 0 5 0 0 8 7 7 *